THE GAS TANK CHRONICLES:

True Tales of My Two Years of Modern Day Circuit Riding

I0107887

Brad K. Zockoll

"The Gas Tank Chronicles are a must-read for anyone who's yearning for the freshness of God's touch, anyone who needs to laugh, and anyone who wants to know that God is still moving, still loving, and still changing people's lives. Brad Zockoll paints true stories filled with depth and humor. Once you begin reading, you won't stop!"
—Susie Shellenberger, Editor
SUSIE Magazine

Other works by Brad Zockoll:

Incident at Jupiter Lighthouse

Guffman's Universe

That Summer with Philip

Risking Daylight

Fugue in D Minor

Fluid Universe

Poincare's Code

Summer Sisterhood

Nowhere, Arizona

Ugly Angel

42nd Street Publishing

ISBN: 978-0615538754 (42nd Street Publishing)

DEDICATION

To my dear Jill, who has been a strong, loving, encouraging and joyful wife for over a quarter of a century.

That's quite a long time to put up with someone like me, so I thought she deserved something nice like this dedication. And probably a dinner at Cracker Barrel.

NOTE TO THE READER:

For the sake of discretion, in all cases I have changed the names of the people involved, and for chronological brevity in some cases I've changed the dates of the actual events within the two year time frame. I assure you, though, that my personal experiences recorded within the pages of this book are true.

I couldn't have made this stuff up if I tried.

CONTENTS

Brad Zockoll

INTRODUCTION

When I was twenty-one, I threw my few belongings into the back of my hideously orange-colored Dodge Aspen and pulled out of Hollister, California. Although I had spent a magnificent two years with the eager youngsters of the local church youth group, I was tired in more ways than one. Worn out, you could say. I needed to head to a new horizon. In many ways those days were extremely hard, and I do not wish to discuss them in this book. I wish, though, to tell you about what I wanted. *Desperately* wanted.

I wanted to see God again.

Working in my life.

Day to day.

Hour by hour.

Minute by minute.

I wanted to know what it would be like to pray - with freedom and boldness - in times of uncharted territory.

I wanted to be able to share the God of the Bible not only in how He worked with others, but how He was – *right now* - working in me.

I wanted to live by faith.

I wanted to see if God could sustain me as I shared His word around the country to churches, schools, assemblies, Bible groups, families, rescue missions ... anybody who would have me.

The kicker was that I would not ask for any money at all.

I made this vow to God, and I was serious about it. No matter how hard the circumstances would be, I would never ask for a dime. If it came to that, I promised I would stop right where I was and get a job and accept the fact that God was done with my journey as a circuit riding messenger.

In other words, I wanted to see how God handled dangerous, tight-wire situations. I wanted to learn even as I taught.

So in my final days in California, I spent over a month and a half writing letters to churches all across the country, telling them I would be traveling through their area on a particular week of the year. When a few responses trickled in, I pulled out a map of the U.S.A., pinned it on my apartment wall, and with a red marker drew a circular route from coast to coast that I would soon travel in my car. Then as more letters steadily came in, I traced a trail that slowly meandered to specific places on a second route. Even more mail - not much, but enough - came in. I made a third route. This was going to be my solo pilgrimage back to the foundations of my faith. No supporting church or organizations. No benefactors. No teammates along the way – I would be on my own. I thought it would last about seven months, eight at the most.

It lasted two years.

For the sake of my providing the impact as powerfully as possible, I'm not going to give you the real names of the churches I attended. I feel that denominational barriers will hurt the purpose of this book, and I don't want that, so I gave the assemblies some generic sounding names. I've also, as I had earlier stated, changed the names of persons. I want you to see the power of the story for what it is – God working through people, places and circumstances to give me twenty-four months on the road that few people will ever experience.

If you see me today, you won't see anything special, believe me. You'll see a motley-looking fellow who talks to himself, has an unnatural craving for Cheez-Its, and is constantly losing stuff. Don't think this made me a superman or, heaven forbid, a celebrity.

But, ah, did I ever see the beginnings of God's blessings in my life. It made me much, much better than I could ever imagine. It started a whole new approach to ministry for me.

In those two years I learned a lot about myself.

I learned even more about prayer.

And did I ever learn about God. Did I *ever*. These are the stories that I want to share with you.

ACKNOWLEDGMENTS

I owe a debt of gratitude to the very talented Mike Carleton not only for his creative work on the cover of this book but for his enthusiasm in the project.

I also thank the Lord for the fine editing work done by Bobby McCoy, who I consider not only a detail-oriented proofreader but also a true Christian friend.

I also want to thank my son Peter Zockoll who kept a keen eye in proofreading as well and is someone whom I believe will be publishing his own works in the future.

I also want to thank my son Nicholas who has been a very powerful encouragement to me, both in words and in deed.

1.

Georgia: Tank, Bees, and a Ride to Remember

As I passed the Interstate 24 sign, I looked over at the passenger seat where my journal and calendar lay open. I reviewed the notations on the pages and took a deep breath.

Okay, Lord, this is really happening. I'm out on the road by myself, totally depending upon you for support.

The 1983 calendar showed me that June was pretty well filled, according to my modest estimates. I'd be speaking and ministering in one location, have a day or two of travel, and then I'd be at another venue, serving where I could, in any way I could.

This was where the rubber meets the road, man. I was going to see America on the grassroots level. No plane or train travel; this would all be by car. No large organization that would oversee my itinerary or send me monetary assistance. I was really, truly, financially and socially on my own.

God and me.

This would be an especially intimate ministry with rural small-town America. A lion's share of my stops would be with tiny congregations that couldn't afford a speaker of any reputation;

they just didn't have the money. Actually, that's how my calendar was filled up so quickly: I didn't ask for a fee, nor did I request traveling expenses. Whatever the church wanted to give me was what I was going to take. That was my vow to the Lord. If they forgot to give anything at all, my promise to the Lord was that I was going to get in the car and head to the next destination until I ran out of money or out of gas or whatever would be an insurmountable obstacle. Then I would settle at that location and get a job. Would it last a year? A month? A week?

I had sold all of my possessions, took the small sum of cash I earned from three flea market visits (surprising how little your earthly possessions are worth) and crammed only the necessities – two suits and about four changes of clothes, along with toiletries and three Bibles - into a large black Army trunk that barely fit into the back of my orange 1976 two- door Dodge Aspen.

Here I was on the road. It hardly seemed real at first. I was setting my own time schedule and paying for things with cash out of my pocket (actually, I hid it in my left sock. I was a bit paranoid about theft. Why I thought keeping money in my sock was any safer, I couldn't tell you). I'd been on the highways since I pulled out of Hollister, California, with two naps at truck stops.

It saved me hotel money.

Here we go, God.

My first stop was in Clarksville, Georgia.

As I crossed the Georgia state line I couldn't help but smile to myself. This was actually a grand return to an old familiar stomping ground for me, tucked in the northeastern section of the state. Clarksville, Georgia was an amazingly loveable place.

It had some simple main roads, lots of thick lush trees, thick hot summers and a solid business-world reputation as a trusted center for excellent craftsmanship in furniture making. My first encounter with Clarksville was as a university student back in 1978, helping out with a small storefront church. Upon arriving in town that very first time, I stopped at a local bakery to get directions and was treated to some free Danish delights, because the owner was happy to "see someone in town trying to do good." I sat there on the front porch, eating an embarrassingly large pastry and realizing that some people are just really, really fine folks.

The storefront church was just as enjoyable. Led by a portly and ever-grinning pastor who went by the nickname "Tank," the congregation was two dozen at its biggest, peopled by women in sundresses, men in jeans, and children with doe eyes and a penchant for saying my one-syllable name (Brad) drawn out in three syllables: "Buh-RAY- ud." I loved every minute of being with them all, especially from their boisterous singing of "Home of the Soul" (this is the honest truth – they sang from a hymn book with shape notes. *Shape notes,* I tell you. I thought that was Civil War era stuff. If you don't know what I'm talking about, give it a Google and see for yourself). Some of my fondest memories, I'm ashamed to say, were of the eye-popping afternoon lunches of fresh greens, pork chops, mashed potatoes, gravy and homemade pies foisted upon me by farm wives whose husbands would regale me with local tales as I filled up on their produce. I still salivate when I reminisce.

Ah, those were some great days when I was in college those years back. Now as I headed back in 1983, Tank had lost forty pounds, gained a new property for the church and was one of the first respondents to ask me to come and speak.

What a great way to start, I thought. *Going back to old friends.*

I had aimed my car for Georgia and whistled as I drove (my radio didn't work. In fact, neither did the air conditioner). This was going to be a nice quiet family reunion of sorts.

Well, not of the sort I expected.

The church had relocated and was now meeting in a new metallic building with a freshly painted sign and a gravel parking lot. The inside of the building still had that smell of new lumber and fresh paint so familiar to all homebuilders. Tank had met me at the door with a firm handshake and a wink, proudly introducing me to the new location and telling me what I longed to hear:

"There's gonna be a nice big spread of food for us all to have after the meetin' tonight, son."

Boy, this circuit-riding thing was starting out better than I thought.

I stepped into the pulpit that Sunday evening with a gracious and comfortable feeling that we were all going to have a grand time in the Word. The congregation had swelled to, oh, about fifty, the people huddled on metal chairs. The smattering of kids comprising the youth group sat on the front row, intent as if I were about to reveal the next NASA space mission. One young couple – I found out their names were Skeeter and Jan - stood in the back of the auditorium, both arms wrapped around each other and smiling blissfully. It was an unusual hug, an odd position that they took: chest–to-chest and knees-to-knees. It made for an uncomfortable casual conversation on my side, but they didn't seem to mind. What was especially noticeable was their firmly locked grip - almost as if they were afraid someone would steal their spouse. All through the evening they stood like that, never letting go. Tank told me they'd been married for two months and still hadn't let go of each other.

And so I was at the pulpit for my first meeting. As I started to share my text in the book of James, however, I encountered a noise that I couldn't decipher.

Me: "Let's turn to the first chapter of James and I –"

Noise: *Whine*

Me: "Um... in the twenty-second verse, there's an exhortation that I want to share with – "

Noise: *Whine whiiiiine*

Me: "- share with you about going the extra step beyond being a mere listener. We should all –"

Noise: *Whine snort whiiiiiiiiiine*

Where was that noise coming from? Nobody seemed to notice the constant interruption ... or at least they were amazingly good at ignoring it. I scanned the audience as I spoke, desperately glancing about to find the source of this high-pitched, hair-raising noise. And I found it. Three rows deep, seven chairs from the left aisle. There he was, a red-haired, freckle-faced kid of about seven, thin as a rail with a face that was even redder than his hair. He was crying, but not in the heart-rending sorrow that can shake a person. This was a long-drawn out continual fingernail-across-the-blackboard screech of a whine that let me know he was in the midst of a self-centered funk. And, brother, that whine was *loud*.

Although I don't know how I did it, I continued laboring through my outline as I assessed the situation. *Surely there must be parents or a guardian about...* and indeed there was, right next to the child. His mother was getting the full blast of this coil of sound but she was totally unresponsive. In fact, Mother sat there with heavy-lidded eyes like she was beyond tired. She was awake - but *out* of it.

This whining continued on a pace of twice a minute through the entire message. And I spoke for twenty-five minutes. This was my first message, and it was a disaster. I stuttered all through it, trying to dodge the mortar-bomb whines that were being lobbed at me by the red-haired kid.

Afterwards I was quite dejected, but amazingly enough nobody seemed a bit bothered by it, nor did they mention it. In fact, to my simmering suspicion, everyone seemed so excited about the food in the back dining hall that everything else – especially the message – was quite forgotten completely.

While people were coming up and shaking my hand, hugging me and patting my shoulder, there was a small call from Amy, Tank's petite daughter. Everyone kept chatting, but I could hear Amy was insistent in needing some help, so I excused myself and walked past Skeeter and Jan who were still standing with both arms wrapped around each other and smiling blissfully. I stepped to the dining hall doorway where Amy stood facing me, her hand on the knob. I actually thought this was a trick, that she would usher me through the doorway to a loud blast of cheering and a huge buffet of food festooned with streamers and ribbons, celebrating my homecoming.

Instead, Amy said, "Brad, we've got bees."

"Oh," I answered emptily. "Uh, are there many of them? Does the church have any spray?" I got a bit bold. "When I was a teen I worked on a few farms, and sometimes they had bees. Here, I'll get them for you."

She shook her head and looked me in the eyes. "Brad, there are a lot of bees." She kept her hand on the doorknob, not moving.

After an uncomfortable minute of staring at each other, I coughed lightly and nodded toward the door. "Well, Amy, why don't I take a look and see what I can do?" She moved aside as I gently turned the doorknob and took a peek.

There were bees, all right.

Lots of bees, like she said. Hundreds ... no, thousands of bees.

Tons of 'em. It was like a scene out of a horror movie. They were streaming through an air duct and were covering, so help me, *covering* every bit of food on the table. They were crawling all over the fried chicken. They were mucking through the icing on the pink sheet cakes. I am not making this up. They were dive-bombing the fruits, ham sandwiches, gravies, and I tell you honestly that some were swimming in the lemonade.

Some of them spotted me.

I stepped back and slammed the door. I looked at Amy and gulped. "Yes, there are a lot of bees."

I looked for Tank, carrying a broken heart. There was no way we were going to have a meal of any kind that night. No biscuits. No blueberry cobbler. Not even a chicken wing. I was quite surprised that nobody else besides Amy had taken time to notice the problem with the dining hall's situation.

I moped toward the middle of the church. "Is Tank around?", I asked the people who were now circled on one corner of the main auditorium. A few turned around and looked at me and smiled slightly. "Yes, Brad, he's right here." They stepped back slightly and I could see that Tank was standing in the same position as the rest of the folks: arms folded, looking down, face grim.

Tank looked at me solemnly and said, "We have a situation, here, Bradley."

I followed his gaze and looked down to the corner of the room.

There was a small brunette woman leaning against the wall, completely unconscious. Her glasses were slightly askew. I recognized her. She was Whiney Boy's mom.

"What happened?" I asked.

"Dunno," Tank answered, stroking his chin and folding his arms again. "She walked over here acting funny an' talking even funnier, an' here she fell."

"She always does that," said a man who had his back to us. He was walking toward a water fountain. I glanced back. It struck me strange that he had said it in so matter-of-fact a manner.

"Who is he?" I asked, wondering why he would know this fact.

"Oh, that's Bobby," said Amy, who also had her arms folded. "Bobby's her husband."

Nobody seemed to share my concern that Bobby was walking around on the other side of the room while his wife was completely unconsciousness. Skeeter and Jan stood off to the side, both arms wrapped around each other and looking a wee bit concerned.

I coughed slightly. "Well, uh, isn't there something we should do?" I realized I was treading on local church etiquette here. I'm the guest; the pastor, deacons or a leader should be taking control of the situation. However, since everyone – and I mean *everyone* – seemed satisfied with hugging themselves (or someone else, as in Skeeter and Jan's case) and looking on, I stooped down and drew near to the woman.

"Can you hear me?"

Her eye faintly flickered but she closed them again. She gave no verbal response.

"Daddy, there's bees in the back room," said Amy.

"Aw," said Tank. "Did they get in the pies?"

"Yes," said Amy. "They did."

I checked the woman's pulse. "What's her name?"

"She's Melody Jean," said a voice.

"She did this three times yesterday," called Bobby.

"Her pulse is steady," I said, placing the back of my hand on her forehead, "and she doesn't seem to have a fever. But we need to get her awake."

A white haired gentleman leaned forward and stuffed something in my hand. "This ought to do it, preacher," he said, smiling. I looked down. He had given me a smelling salt tablet.

Shaking my head slightly at the thought of why someone would mosey around town with smelling salts in their pocket, I broke it and waved it under Melody Jean's nose. Her eyes opened widely and she shuddered, but then within ten seconds she closed her eyelids and fell back against the wall with a *thunk*.

"She woke and then she fainted again, Bobby," called Tank.

"Well, what am I supposed to do about it?" asked Bobby.

9

"Hey preacher," said the white-haired gentleman. "Stick it up her nose. That'll do it. Way up."

I shrugged and lifted the smelling salts tablet up into the edge of her nostril.

"Naw, shove it *way* up there," he said.

I inserted the tablet as far as I dared in a social setting, and her eyes blazed open in a cartoon-like manner... before she passed out again.

"She fainted again, Daddy," said Amy.

"I saw that," said Tank.

"Look," I said, turning around while still on one knee, "we've got to get her to an emergency room. This is obviously not normal. She needs help."

"I agree," said a lady to my right. "I'm a nurse and I should know." She never moved, though.

I blinked three times.

"Let's lift her up an' get her to a car," Tank said, and I grabbed her under one arm while Tank reached for the other. She oozed out from under our grasp like Jello under a hot sun. I realized that in this genteel setting it might be embarrassing to see how we could grapple with a woman who suddenly has become fluid to the touch.

"Uh," I said, but Tank already had the same thought.

"Bobby," he called over his shoulder, "come over here an' get your wife."

Bobby obeyed but started whining. "And what am I supposed to do with her, Tank?" I could see where Whiney Boy got his habit.

Tank straightened up. "You're gonna go get your car an' you're gonna take her over the hill to the Toccoa hospital, that's what you're gonna do."

Bobby shrugged and strode through the group and, so help me, in one swooping motion he threw her over his back in a fireman's carry. "Okay, then, get out of the way. Andy, hand me my keys. They're over there on that red chair."

The rest of the group watched as he lumbered out into the parking lot toward a tan station wagon with a rusty fender. "Now, how am I supposed to get her in?" He looked like he was going to toss her in the back compartment through the window.

"Here, I'll help," I said as I sprinted forward. "Not the back cargo area, Bobby, put her here, right behind the driver's seat." We pulled her into the dusty vinyl back seat. Thankfully, she was small enough to lie completely across with her head on the armrest. "I better come and help," said Amy, sliding into the passenger seat. Mumbling, Bobby fell heavily into the front seat and started the car. As soon as he put the car in gear and moved it, Melody Jean rolled off the seat and onto the floorboard with another *thunk*. The rest of the church folded their arms and watched. Skeeter and Jan, both arms wrapped tightly around each other, shook their heads in disapproval.

"Uh, look," I said. "She's not going to be able to make it to the hospital like this." I pulled down the back hatch and with a grunt, climbed into the cargo of the station wagon, pulled off my suit jacket and reached over. Amy leaned over from her position in the front and we hauled Melody Jean back up on the seat.

"Well, are you ready?" Bobby asked with a tinge of irritation evident in his voice. I looked down at Melody Jean, who was ready to roll over again. The only solution I could think of was to lean bodily over the seat and hold her by the wrist with one of my hands while cradling her head with my other hand. Mind you, I am kneeling in the cargo area and leaning over the seat doing this. My knees are in the back section, where the kiddies and the flowerpots are usually thrown.

Bobby gave a half-hearted wave to the people in the parking lot and threw on his turn signal blinker as he entered the main road.

"I just don't get her sometimes," he said aloud, while dribbling along at 22 miles per hour in a 40 m.p.h. zone. "She does this stuff, like, every day lately."

"Well, Bobby," said Amy. "You ought to look out after her, make sure she don't have a cold or headache or something."

Bobby shrugged and glanced over at the convenient mart with a sign for corn dogs. For the life of me, I really thought he was thinking about pulling in and getting a soft drink and a dog.

Melody Jean stirred. "Arrrr*aaaaaaaaaaah*," she groaned piteously. I grew nervous. She was getting pale and this guy was puttering as slow as if we were sight-seeing.

But that noise caught his attention.

"What was that?" Bobby snapped his head around. That's when I decided to make my big dramatic statement.

"She's *sick*, Bobby," I said as sternly as I could. "Can't you see that? This is *not normal*. Your wife is very, *very* sick. People don't just up and faint in public, man. They don't plop down and remain unresponsive. There is something," I bobbed my head for emphasis, "*seriously, seriously* wrong with your wife."

That was my speech. In reflection, I should not have made it so forceful. Upon further reflection, I was an absolute idiot to get the driver stirred up.

The expression across his face was as if he had stuck his finger into a light socket. His eyebrows went up and his neck went stiff. And his foot crammed on the accelerator. *Crammed.*

The only thing that kept me from sliding out the back gate was the fact that I was holding onto Melody Jean. In fact, I suddenly realized that I was actually *clinging* to her as we shot through the town. I do not embellish when I tell you from my vantage point that the speedometer said we were clearing seventy. Within the town limits.

Bobby was now stammering and glancing back towards her. "I – I just had no idea... I didn't realize..."

His right hand locked on the steering wheel, his left arm was cocked up at the elbow, with his raised hand furiously twitching into an open–and-closed fist rhythm. He looked in the back, full in her face. "Is she gonna make it?"

I gulped. He was racing towards the back of a stationary car sitting at an intersection. I tried to stay calm. "Bobby, she'll be fine if you get us to the hospital *in one piece.* Now, keep your eye on the road." He zoomed around the car ahead and weaved like a stock car driver on the last lap.

We cleared the city limits and headed up the hill. The speedometer said eighty. There were cars in both lanes, doing approximately thirty-five miles per hour. Bobby was looking back at long intervals, staring at his wife. With deep horror I realized that I was not only without a seat belt, I was on my knees, leaning over the back seat and in the worst possible position for an accident. If Bobby should slam into another car from behind, the deceleration would give me enough forward inertia to torpedo me right by Amy's ear and through the windshield.

"Bobby, mind the car ahead of you," said Amy quietly. He swerved, missing it by inches. He looked back, gripping and ungripping his hand. "Ah, she's gonna die, I just know it." A fully stopped car was in front of us, and Bobby didn't see it.

"Another car," said Amy, pointing.

Bobby snapped his head around, swung the car so hard that I slid and hit the cargo area's side wall with my hip while still hanging on. When the speedometer said ninety miles per hour, I decided not to look any more. We zipped and swerved through traffic like a skier in an Olympic slalom course. More than once there could not have been a half-foot clearance between our car and the bumper of other vehicles.

Up ahead was the hospital, but Bobby kept looking back. Not glancing, mind you, but *staring* at her.

"*Bobby*," I called loudly, because we were well past the stage of politeness. Shouting was the only thing to get through to him. "The hospital is up here on the left, and that sign is pointing to the Emergency Room entrance. You see it? Look at it. Bobby, you've got to *slow down* to make this turn, and make the turn across the highway in front of traffic, okay? There is traffic coming toward us, and so *you must slow down*."

He went into a slide that would have made any drift racing driver proud. We screeched past a dump truck, bounced into the entrance and jostled over speed bumps before sliding onto the porch that was the entrance to the ER. Profuse with thanks to the Heavenly Father for journeying mercy, I was trying to unfold myself from the back as I saw Bobby get out and sprint. His panic mode was so extreme that in a fit of energy, he got out and began running. Not toward the entrance. Not toward one of the medical staff. Just running.

I rolled out of the back of the station wagon as I heard one of the ER attendants, a skinny fellow with a shock of uncombed yellow hair speak in a slow drawl as he pointed listlessly toward Melody Jean. "D'ye need a gurney or a wheelchair?" The other attendant, a stocky fellow with sleepy eyes, looked on disinterestedly.

"Um," I said, rubbing my hip and overcoming a state of shock, "this woman fainted in a meeting and we can't bring her around..."

"D'ye want a gurney or a wheelchair?"

"Fellas," I said, straightening up. "*You're* the professionals, and you can see this woman is out cold, so I think..."

"D'ye want a gurney or a wheelchair?" asked Blondie a third time.

To my left I heard an explosive noise that was, shockingly, emanating from a human. It was mean. It was deep.

It was *Amy.*

Gone was the deep Georgia genteel attitude. Bobby's erratic behavior, the bees, and the ride had changed her. Her eyes were flaring and her hair had that static-on-a-cat look. Her voice was razor sharp, coming through clenched teeth. She ripped through her words like a lumberjack's crosscut saw on a redwood tree.

"There is a *woman* in this *car* who *collapsed* and is *unresponsive.* She could be *dying* so you're going to *get* her out of that *car* and *get* her help *right now,* d'y'hear? *NOW.*"

Blondie snapped to attention. "We'll get a gurney." They darted back into the building and had Melody Jean wheeled through the doors within seconds.

With shaky legs I wandered over to the admission window where I found Tank leaning casually on the counter, and wonder of wonders, Bobby. Bobby was openly crying while rifling through all of the cards in his wallet, looking for his Blue Cross card. He couldn't find it, though he was rapidly shuffling cards like a Las Vegas dealer.

Sorting through the thick stack madly, he was whining and snuffling. "I don't know what I'd do with the kids, Tank, if she dies." He shuffled yet a third time. "I can't find the Blue Cross card, just can't find it. Tank, if she dies I can't take care of the kids."

The matronly attendant behind the counter sipped a diet Coke and waited patiently.

Bobby was on his fourth try when Tank reached over casually, pulled out the Blue Cross card and handed it to the attendant. Bobby had shuffled by it three times without really looking at it. Now he grabbed the hair just over his forehead and wept. Tank looked over his head with a faraway gaze.

"You understand," sobbed Bobby, "I got enough stuff to do around the house. I can't take care of the kids, Tank. What'll I do if'n she dies?"

Tank kept that faraway look.

"I got the truck payments and a promotion due me," continued Bobby. "The kids'll need to be driven to school every day..."

Tank kept his gaze, but finally spoke. "Aw, Bobby, hush up," he said. "Melody Jean ain't gonna die. Now come on over here an' sit down. The Falcons are playin' on the television. Let's sit and watch the game."

I looked up over my shoulder. Tank's faraway gaze was locked on the waiting room TV. The NFL game was on, and indeed, the Atlanta Falcons were in full battle.

Bobby turned and squinted at the television. "Oh," he said. "Well, okay." He wandered over to a seat and plopped down. That was the last I saw of him.

Things seemed to be in hand, so I glanced at my watch and realized that it was time for me to head to my car. A kindly man had grabbed my keys and driven my car to the hospital, following Bobby's station wagon. "You was driving real fast and dangerous," he chided me kindly while he handed me my keys. "Gotta be careful next time. Coulda been killed."

I thanked him and walked into the waiting room. As I walked through the hallway, I realized that Tank had not taken an offering during the service and since we had no supper afterwards, he may have forgotten to give me an honorarium. I would get no offering or traveling expenses for this cross-country trip.

My first test, Lord. Okay, then. I know You'll take care of me. I made a promise not to ask. I breathed deeply and realized that I was truly at peace. God *would* take care of me. I relaxed and smiled.

The entire congregation was standing in the lobby, arms folded and chatting happily as if we were about to embark on a picnic on the front lawn of the hospital. Amy stepped forward as the whole group turned and grinned at me.

"The doctor just came out and told us," Amy exclaimed. "Guess what! Melody Jean's gonna have a baby! They've got her safe and taken care of! A little 'un!"

I shook my head and grinned widely. "Well, what do you know! That's great news, it really is." Amy reached out and took my hand with both hers. She shook it and said, "Brad, the ladies of the church left a small gift in the back of your car as a thank you for all you've done. Come again soon, okay?"

"I will, as soon as I'm able." I stepped back and drew a long breath, still trying to take in what had happened in the last few hours. "Well, since I know she's okay," I said, pulling on my suit coat, "I guess I must be going now. I need to head up north – Delaware and Maryland are my next stops."

The people murmured their thanks and drew close to me. Amidst back-pats, hugs and handshakes – along with a deep grief of not having any cherry pie, corn on the cob or roast beef due to the bees – I walked out to the car and waved goodbye.

"Oh, hey, son," Tank waved and jogged toward the car as I was about to close the door. "We passed the hat for you." I later calculated that it was - to the dollar - enough gas money to get me to my next church in Bel Air, Maryland.

I looked behind me as I backed the Aspen out of the parking space, but pulled the car to a sudden stop. Settled atop my Army trunk and crammed into the floorboards were packages and boxes of homemade foods, ranging from biscuits to jars of honey to Tupperware containers loaded with fried chicken. And not a bee in sight.

I looked up at the hospital entrance in shock. Tank and Amy stood laughing and waving. "We had some of the ladies run home on the way to the hospital and get you some fresh goodies on the road," called Amy. "I *told* you we had a small gift for you!"

I smiled as I drifted out of the parking lot, waving to Tank and Amy as they stepped back into the hospital, assuring myself of God's close hand in all that was done, especially in seeing that I was able to survive a trip in Bobby's station wagon.

What a great way to start my circuit riding. What a great way for God to say, "Welcome to a new ministry."

Before turning onto the highway, I gave one final glance in the rear-view mirror and had a good long laugh because...

...my last sight of the congregation was of Skeeter and Jan standing on the steps of the hospital, both arms wrapped around each other and smiling blissfully.

P.S. I received a letter from Tank a month later. Melody Jean gave birth to a fine seven-pound, eleven-ounce boy.

2.

Delaware: Truck Stops, Nuns, and a Dent in the Head

I was on my way to Delaware after a short speaking engagement in Bel Air, Maryland. I was a bit groggy, but I figured that I'd better get used to it if I was going to keep up the schedule I had created. After leaving Georgia, my first night's stop had been snoozing in the front seat of my car between two semi-tractor trailers at a Virginia Flying J truck stop (Flying J would become an inexpensive home-away-from-home for me in the coming months. I also developed an affinity for some other truck stops as well: Love's Travel Centers had excellent coffee, and TravelCenters of America seem to populate their stores with toothy-grinned, extra-friendly people), with one leg draped over the steering wheel. I was not ignorant of the crimes that were committed in rest stops and truck stops along the highway, so I came up with the idea that if someone were to try to break into my car, I would simply shift my leg and step on the car horn. It must have been an intimidating sight, for I can freely assure you that not once in my two years of travel did I ever once become a victim of a robbery at a Flying J.

My time in Bel Air had been an adventure in itself. In the first place, the meetings were delightful; I met wonderful people at First Bible Church who were intensely interested in the Scriptures and sought every opportunity to corner me in order to ask questions after each message. Well, now that I think about it, either they were intensely interested, or I botched up the message so bad that they needed help in sorting out what I had just said.

Pastor Ainsley Curtis was a gracious host as well as a part-time farmer, so I was able to enjoy a rural retreat whenever we weren't working at the church. In all seriousness, I really did find the congregation active, responsive and positive – the kind of reception any speaker would enjoy. As I shared Christ's words of the Sermon on the Mount passage in the book of Matthew, there was a visible and encouraging movement among the folk, wanting to make these things *real* in their lives, and through the week they'd give testimony on how they'd been working at it.

God was truly moving among the little congregation, and it was refreshing for me to see people *activating* the Scriptures, if I may coin a phrase. From visiting the elderly and infirm to openly talking about Christ with their friends and relatives, they were truly go-getters. Spectators these people weren't – within their own little parts of the world, they were showing a real-life example of the old song "Brighten the Corner Where You Are."

This was a particularly memorable series of church services, because the church was meeting in an Odd Fellows' Hall. Full of nooks and crannies, the Hall was a place of intrigue to all of the younger folks, and they got a kick out of the church renting space here. I got curious myself, truth be told. After the morning service some of the teen boys called me aside and showed me an unlocked out-of-the-way closet. It held a full rack of shiny robes and heavy necklaces that must've been the officiates' garb worn at meetings of the organization. I can't say that I know much about the Odd Fellows, so I don't want to be casting a pall over them, but I must admit, there was an aura of mystery about the whole place. I got a kick out of seeing the costumes, but the ultimate surprise to me when they showed me a hidden square-inch sliding panel that allowed at secretive look in on the proceedings of a meeting. What kind of cloak and dagger activities went on in here?

As I had said, the meetings themselves were great. It was *after* the services when I found that things would get a bit rough for me.
I had endured a fitful first night while staying in the Curtis farmyard in a twelve-foot trailer, located a good football field's distance away from the farmhouse. On that first night I woke to a frenetic buzzing and pulled open a closet door to find a melon-sized hornets' nest on the *inside* of the trailer. The now-angry hornets responded unkindly to my intrusion, and the only thing from an unimaginable attack – I am not making this up – was in me frantically grabbing a can of mace I had stored in my back pack. Three shots put the whole colony on the floor. It also drove me from the trailer. I had to move outside for an hour, sitting in the dark, red leaky eyes and all.

The next day was exhausting. Besides doing in-town visitation to some needy folk and some counseling to a few young people, Pastor Curtis and I took time to put on old clothes, get out some tools and do a little preventative maintenance on my mode of transportation. The whole afternoon was filled with his quiet gasps as we worked on the engine and slid beneath the car. He was totally dumbfounded that the Aspen hadn't fallen apart on me, or even how I could manage to survive in such a decrepit vehicle. The afternoon conversations went something like this:

Pastor: "Well, I think you ought to consider more freon for the air conditioner, son."

Me: "That's okay, pastor. The air conditioner doesn't work."

Pastor: *small gasp*

Me: "I'll be heading into Delaware after this, so the ride won't be too long."

Pastor: "Well, even on long trips, your radio will keep you awake. Do you have any favorite Christian radio stations?"

Me: "No, sir, the radio doesn't work either."

Pastor: *small gasp*

Me: Well, I guess I'm a quart low of oil. I'll take care of that.

Pastor: I guess I don't even need to ask you if you have a jack in case you get a flat tire.

Me: Uh, no.

Pastor: *small gasp*

I fell into bed that night, worn and weary from all the day's activity. I would be speaking three times the next day, so I was eager to get a good night's rest. It was while I was sleeping soundly that night that the stillness of the barnyard was cut by an urgent knocking on the door.

There has always been a strange thing about me when it comes to being brought out of a deep sleep. When I'm awakened in this manner, I'm instantly and fully alert – at least for a minute and a half.

Knock knock knock knock BANG BANG BANG

I threw my covers off and shot up to a sitting position, wide-eyed.

"Yes? What is it?" I called.

"Brother Brad, this is Beatrice."

My mind clicked and the name registered in an instant. I remembered a girl named Beatrice from the meetings the previous day. She was a dark-haired willowy girl about my age, and she reminded me of an owl for two reasons: her head constantly swiveled back and forth when she talked with people, and she suffered from insomnia, mostly from a childhood fear of the dark. The pastor assured me he was not exaggerating when he had told me she averaged over thirty cups of coffee a night. *She must be on an important mission to be crossing an unlit field at this time of night.*

"Brother Brad," Beatrice called through the trailer door, "my daddy's coming out of surgery within the hour and we think the doctor may say that he has incurable cancer. My whole family's over at St. Mary's. Would you come to the hospital and be with us when the doctor breaks us the news? We need the support and I can't get Pastor Curtis to answer his door."

"Uh, sure. Give me a minute or two so I –"

"The directions are on the front porch of the main house," she called as I heard her voice fading and her footsteps running away. "Taped to the screen door. I gotta go. Please hurry."

I called loudly as I ran my hand through my hair. "Right. Okay. On my way."

I stumbled about in the little trailer (avoiding the dead hornets on the floor) and threw on a hooded sweatshirt and some old jeans as quickly as possible. I didn't even take time to comb my hair – this sounded pretty urgent. The Aspen bounced and jostled across the field as I drove to the farmhouse and pulled up to the front. Sure enough, Beatrice had left directions taped to the screen door. I grabbed the paper, and, with a flashlight in the interior of the car, (my Aspen's interior light bulb had broken long ago. I forgot to mention that to the pastor) I sped to St. Mary's Hospital.

I didn't know how late it was whenever I pulled my car into a space at the hospital and made my way to the entrance. I was pretty bleary and in need of about a gallon of coffee. Better yet, I could've just chewed the unbrewed coffee beans, I was that tired. My alertness had worn off, and I was getting kind of wobbly.

"Hello, I'm clergy ... I guess... yes," I said at the receptionist's table which was marked 'Patient Information.'" I rubbed my eye and cleared my throat and tried to put any sort of formal words together. "Um, let's see. Could you direct me? For I need help, you see. I'm here to be with Beatrice's family. At this time of need. In their lives." I sounded like a Grade A undiluted imbecile.

The older lady behind the desk looked at my oversized hooded sweatshirt and patched jeans and smiled benevolently. "Well, yes, certainly. They're right over there, sir," she said, pointing to a huddled group. "Here, why don't I walk you over?"

I was escorted over in the vicinity of the family who stood together, talking lowly. I started to approach the group when Beatrice came over and waved her hands.

"There's no need for you to come over right now, Brother Brad, because the family's making, er... arrangements, in case ... well..." she crinkled her eyes and swiveled her head, "... *you know*. Look, I'll call you when the doctor comes out and gives us the news. We'll need you to be ready, okay?" With that, she turned on her heel quickly and strode back to the family meeting.

Not knowing what to do, I shrugged and shuffled over to a secondary waiting room, a cool quiet room with a long wall of glass and a crucifix just inside its entrance; *Yes, this was a Catholic Hospital*, I remembered. I was impressed at how orderly and neat everything was. The St. Mary's people really made sure their visiting friends and family were made as comfortable as possible, I realized as I settled into one of the nicest, softest sectional sofas ever placed in a hospital waiting room.

I closed my eyes and I was relaxed quite deeply. And I fell asleep. No, it's better to say that I was out.

Out.

Dead-to-the-world, brain-shut-down *out.*

I was so far into miles-deep slumber that I don't remember dreaming at all. I was sawing logs like nobody's business, and drifting farther and farther away from this world.

In the middle of my deepest delta stage of sleep, I heard a small cough in front of me. As I said, whenever I hear a noise, I usually pop right up and am responsive.

Well, not this time.

Oh, I was awake immediately all right, but when I looked ahead of me I was looking straight into the face of a white-and-black robed figure.

A nun, about fifty years of age with cat-eye glasses, was wearing one of the most saintly and sweet faces I had ever seen.

"May I help you?" she asked softly.

I blinked, totally confused. *Where was I?*

The nun took up my whole line of vision – she must have been standing only about two feet from me, so as I looked up in my crumpled position, I was awed by the presence. There was quiet ambient music in the background. Soothing stuff.

The music. Her robes. Is she an angel?

Have I died?

"I...uh..." I was unable to communicate. Who *was* she?

I looked around. A nice well-lit room... a cross... a comfortable place to rest... *am I in Heaven?*

She turned her head to one side. "Is there someone here you wish to see?"

I stared hard at her. *Get your thoughts together, boy. If this really* **was** *heaven, this angel would have a pretty good idea of Who I'd wish to see. Waaaaait a minute, now...since when did angels wear out-of-date glasses? Why would they need glasses?*

That was actually my reasoning, so you could tell I was in a pretty deep stupor. I rubbed the top of my scalp slowly, mumbling to myself. I wouldn't give up, though, fighting to get awake and reason this out before I moved a muscle. Then it hit me, sprinting to the reasoning and rational part of my skull. *Hospital. Family. Dad's in an operation.*

The fog wouldn't go away, though. I looked over and saw the family still huddled and talking. "I'm ... well, I am clergy. I'm with them, those people ... over there." I gave a half-hearted gesture in their direction.

The nun took a long look at my clothing and smiled a little less. "And what are their names?" she asked gently but crisply.

I was blank. I had no idea what Beatrice's last name was. In fact, at this time of the night, I couldn't even remember Beatrice's *first* name. Again, I pointed weakly. I am not making this up. I pointed over toward them and said simply: "Th-them. Those people. There."

The nun looked at the family, who coincidentally had their backs to me and were still talking animatedly. She turned around and looked at me, this time with no smile at all. I figured out what was in her mind: *A homeless guy wanders in here to steal a little sleep, pretending he's with a nearby family. A crasher.*

She reached out to take my hand and lead me out the door, and I had no way to explain myself. Thankfully, Beatrice came over at that instant. "Brother Brad, would you come over and sit with us now? The doctor's going to talk with us."

The nun glanced at Beatrice, leveled a long authoritarian stare at me and turned quietly away. To this day I believe that she thought that Beatrice was showing benevolence to an uncombed homeless man trying to get a waiting room nap. However, I was led to the family, who amazingly enough treated me with the utmost ministerial respect despite the fact that I looked like Larry Fine of the Three Stooges.

P.S. Beatrice's dad was free of cancer.

My hospital incident was the beginning of a series of events that began putting a new lesson in my heart: *I had better have a good sense of humor about myself.* Humility is a powerful part of a person's ministry, and with the humble attitude comes an ability to laugh at oneself, no matter how embarrassing the situation. This was a good thing to understand as soon as possible, for from the first day in Clarksville, Georgia to my final days when I finally puttered to a stop in central Ohio, something unpredictable and unusual continually happened on the circuit.

To me.

Through the time I was on the journey, I realized that I was going find myself in situations where I had absolutely no control, and not only would I totally rely upon the Lord Jesus for instruction and peace, I had to rely upon Him to give me the spirit of self-effacement.

One of the most pointed lessons I began learning was that I didn't have natural gift of gab that I would like to think I had. I was soon to learn that I would often be faced with a situation where I just couldn't think of anything to say. This was hard for me, because my first years of college were in pursuit of a radio broadcasting degree, where talk was my strong point – at least in my opinion. Since my childhood I had wanted to be a radio announcer or possibly an anchorman of a television news station, and in fact, as a high school student I had taken a few jobs as an emcee for social events and some stints as a radio disc jockey. I even gave the morning announcements over the school's P.A. system each school day. I prided myself on having the right presentation and responses, always ready for a quip and a laugh.

Well, I soon found out that I would end up speechless more than one time, brother.

It became increasingly clear to me that God was going to tear down my self-sufficient pride in this area and many times put the laugh on me.

Later that very week I was walking through the streets of the small town of Crisfield, Maryland, joining the youth group in inviting people to the Coastal Church's service that evening. For the most part, we received some very polite responses, but once in a while we'd run into a disagreeable sort of person. After about an hour of chatting with folks on the street, some of the youth group members sent word to me that a man in front of the mom-and-pop candy store was very agitated and frightening one of the church girls. I trotted over to where Sarah stood smiling nervously and looking to me for help. The lean man in front of her appeared to be in his late sixties, wearing a wide battered cowboy hat and blue jeans. He was rattling on, pointing at her and barking out his words in machine-gun rapidity.

"Hi, friend," I said loudly as I stepped up to him. "Anything I can do for you?"

He wheeled and faced me. "Now, I'm gonna tell you just what I tol' her. I wuz tellin' her that I don't need to talk about Heaven, I already faced death oncet."

Yes, he did say "oncet."

"That so?" I said, trying to calm him down. "And did it help you see the need for preparing for eternity?" I was trying to make a smooth transition here. Maybe I could help guide him to do some serious thinking...

He plowed ahead. "Few years ago it was - two years ago, to be exact – yeah, that was when I had it happen to me. Three guys caught up to me when I was coming home from doin' some shopping down at the Git Your Grub convenient mart. Well, they were set to rob me when the time was right. I walked on a piece and that's when they made their move. They pulled me into an alley and in order to git my money, they busted my head with a lead pipe. It put a hole right in my head, one inch deep. Cracked a dent in my skull, I tell you." He pointed to the area underneath his cowboy hat where the injury would have been.

Sarah stepped back. I nodded. "I see. And so this really made you –"

Instantly, he whipped off the hat and pointed to the right side of his head, and to my utter horror, there indeed was a two-inch trapezoid-shaped piece of his head indented almost a full inch into his skull. *A full inch.* The skin followed the form perfectly. It was like looking at a satellite image of the moon near the Sea of Tranquility crater.

I was stunned and yet intrigued at the same time. I didn't think it was humanly possible to have a scalp that took on the form of a section of the Grand Canyon. Sarah trotted backwards, but I stayed rooted where I was, still stunned. He waited for my response, and true to form, I gave it to him. In all of my training and preparation for a moment like this, I could only sputter out:

"Hey, th-that's pretty cool."

I don't know why I said it, but I do know that it didn't get the response I would have like to have had for us to continue and talk about spiritual things. I guess few people would like to know that an indentation in their skull is considered "cool."

So much for my mastery of the comeback.

Sarah heard my response, and of course, so did the whole church within a few hours. I was the recipient of more than one snicker among the congregation for my "cool" comment. One man even asked if I had other mod responses ("neat," "wow", or even "gnarly") to other injuries or ailments I'd seen.

Despite my embarrassment, I always tried to steer away from what I call Christian clichés. To this day I strive hard to keep away from what you might call "Believer's Buzzwords", so often the source of confusion to many folks. I soon learned people, no matter where they lived, would go blank if I used the words and phrases so familiar to the Christian world: *sanctification, regeneration, personal relationship and "shadow of a doubt",* to name a few.

I make it a point to teach this important lesson in my classrooms and other teaching opportunities. Last year, while guiding a college Bible study in my home, I told the guys and girls it was once again time for our debate. They laughed, groaned and sat forward, ready to go to battle. We do this about once a month, where I play a non-believer – sometimes a cult member – and we have a spirited round of nose-to-nose debates about the validity of the Bible, the truth of the existence of God, or the explanation of the plan of salvation. I do it to sharpen their skills Biblical apologetics, and although it gets quite animated and even testy at times, it's the favorite part of the evening for the group.

Tonight, I told them, I would play the part of a college freshmen who was a non-Christian seeking to get answers from the rest of the Christians in the room. In our room that night was Jonathan, a brash young man who was a newcomer to our Bible study. Jonathan was a religion major at a local college who felt it necessary to make comments or even corrections at every turn. He was attending with his girlfriend, and I noticed his eyes light up when I said we were going to have this "debate", with me playing the role of the non-believer. He saw this as his chance to shine.

I began with opening remarks challenging them to understand why I felt Christianity was confusing. The exchange between the two sides started picking up speed. As I played the role of the non-theist, the other fellows were carefully and tactfully trying to lay a Biblical foundation for the discussion, but the visitor Jonathan broke in and launched into a brusque presentation:

"Well, now, let's go over the four things you need to have in order to find salvation and sanctification. One, you need to understand the regenerative power of the Holy Spirit in your life, able to make you clean before a God Who cannot accept you as you are. This comes from the mediator Jesus Christ..."

He wasn't even looking at me eye-to-eye. He was gazing at a point about a foot and a half over my head, pulling this narrative from rote memory.

I cut him off, ready to challenge him. Playing the part of the non-Christian, I said, "I have no idea what you're talking about.

You're trying to humiliate me, aren't you? You Christians use terms that none of us can understand. Do you people have some secret language? Are you trying to show you're better than us?"

The students around the room nodded their heads. They understood the lesson I was giving. Not the newcomer. Instead of slowing down and explaining what he meant, he became agitated, so I called a "time-out" and explained why I reacted the way I did – the clichés often confused people. I gave him some examples from personal experience early in my ministry, where people would often become confused and just walk away. However, even after a gentle explanation on the dangers of wordiness and cliché-throwing, he set his jaw and looked away. It was apparent that his pride was hurt. We never saw him again.

Still, I hold to the fact that our speech ought to be understandable. The reason I'm so direct on this is because it was a lesson I learned while traveling on the circuit. As clear as I tried to make the plan of salvation, more than once on my circuit I had someone look up at me with a blank expression and shake their head, telling me clearly, *I don't get what you're saying.* It took a good dose of humility and the growing ability to put myself in their shoes to understand how to explain things without using "high church" words. It was my fault and I worked at being more "human" in my conversation.

Yes, God was grabbing hold of my speech and refining it in all areas of my life. I am sure that the Lord was giving me a pretty straightforward message: *You'll see great things as you serve Me. It is very important, though, to make sure that I am the One who makes this all happen. Don't let your personality get in the way. Oh, and get rid of clichés. Nobody likes them.*

Time to put careful thought into everything you say, rather than letting your speech go running on automatic pilot.

I repeated that in my mind: *Don't run on verbal automatic pilot.*

This became clear to me the next day as I prepared to speak in Laurel, Delaware.

Another unique situation.

I was the guest speaker with Faith Assembly, a small group of folks that held services in a funeral home.

Yes. A funeral home.

Hey, it was a nice well-cared-for facility that was also (ahem) quiet. I actually didn't mind the venue too much except for one thing: the church pulpit was angled in a curious way so that from where I spoke I could see through to the Coffin Display Room –that's where you go to do your shopping and make your selections for burial services. Well, it kept my mind on the hereafter, that's for sure.

The meeting place was unusual enough, but the most memorable part of that meeting was what took place because the pastor himself wasn't at the meeting. Pastor Phil Johnston had contacted me by mail and, with a wide and enthusiastic style of handwriting, asked me to fill in for him while he was away on vacation, assuring me that the church deacons would handle all the other functions of the service. I had arrived at the designated time for the church's evening service and was met by a portly, happy-go-lucky deacon named Dutch, who shook my hand in a bone-crushing grip and happily ushered me into the back of the main room (they had moved the funeral flowers and other accoutrements of anyone deceased, thankfully) where, to my surprise, the congregation of fifty people were sitting and ready for the service.

"They're a-ready for you, preacher," smiled Dutch, grasping my hand and breaking a few more bones. "Have at 'em."

I smiled and asked in a low whisper: "Who is in charge of the overall service? I mean, who will be leading the music? Perhaps he'll want to know the theme of my message and -"

Dutch happily interrupted me and walked me to the front. "Aw, you don't need to worry about coordinating that. You'll be leading the singing yourself." He said it grandly as if he were handing me the choice turkey leg at Thanksgiving.

I did a double take. "Me?"

He nodded. "Yessir, that's about the size of it." He turned and found his seat on the front row, parking his ample self on the edge as if I were going to suddenly go into card tricks and a tap dance. In fact, I'm not sure what kind of a summary was given about me beforehand by the pastor, but the whole congregation looked as if I were St. Augustine or even Billy Graham in the making. Each face had an expectant visage that showed an anticipation that made me uneasy.

Lord, I'm not sure exactly what they want beyond Your Word. Please prepare me.

I looked about and picked up a hymn book on the podium. I had absolutely no preparation time for this. In the dead (pardon the pun) of the room, the group looked at me in eager anticipation. They were ready to sing.

Now, I need you to know why I elaborate on this scene. Those who know me well understand that I am not a gifted singer.

I'm not even a good singer. To tell you the truth, I'm not even a *mediocre* singer.

This'll give you an idea: at my college graduation my class sang a convocation hymn to open the ceremony.

This was one time where I opened up the vocal chords, brother. Overcome by the pomp and joyousness of the occasion, in my excitement about getting my degree and starting my career, I let loose in what I thought was a grand singing voice, a lot louder than usual. A *whole* lot louder, in fact. The students in front of me actually turned around and looked at me, grimacing. If you want something to shatter your musical self-esteem, you need to have people look at you after your singing and grimace. *Grimace.* Grimace is the face you make when you break your leg. It does wonders for your confidence, believe me.

In another situation during my college years – and this is the absolute truth – in a South Carolina Sunday service, I was unexpectedly called upon by rural pastor Bobby Jinkins to come up to the front of the hand-hewn communion table to sing a solo during the altar call. He had figured all of his interns had an operatic voice.

The others did. I didn't.

He gave no warning, and in the emotion of the altar-call invitation time of the service, he had everyone bow their head.

"Listen, y'all. I need you to concentrate on how God can work in you, if you'd just let Him," Pastor Bobby said. "Think now, don't sing." He waved a hand toward me. "Look, I'm gonna have Brad come up here and sing two verses of 'Is Your All on the Altar' while you just meditate. Bradley?"

Sweat broke out on the back of my neck. He *couldn't* mean me. But he did, and there he was, motioning me toward the front.

Look, even on a good day, the best of singers find this particular hymn a challenge. It's the roller coaster of hymns: up, down, all over the scale. The chances of me singing it successfully were like the odds of a middle-school wrestler winning against Andre the Giant in a no-holds-barred cage match.

I gave it my best, though.

And oh, how bad my best was.

As I lilted and strained to the best of my ability, I noticed that my piano player – a fellow student named Pete - was bowing deeply as he played the tune. I thought he was praying. It was only after the service that he told me that he was laughing uncontrollably. I am not making this up.

That was then. This is now, in the funeral home. Seems like the same problem coming up.

Now I am standing in a Delaware funeral home, about to lead the singing. I coughed and smiled at the congregation as if I knew what I was doing. "Good evening, friends. Let's start out and open the service by singing number-"

I flicked quickly through the pages. I hadn't thought of what we were going to sing. "- number 129 in your hymnbook: *He Arose.*" That was a great hymn. Yeah, it would work. It seemed safe.

I lifted my arm both to invite the congregation to stand and to give the pianist the cue. I swept my arm downward and began singing strongly, since there was no PA system. Didn't matter; the people responded. So far, so good. I became louder. We entered into the chorus:

Up from the grave He arose,

With a mighty triumph o'er His foes...

Something went wrong – I was more concerned about volume and tempo than about the words, and I went on verbal automatic pilot. This was a problem because of a bad event back in college. Let me explain.

At my Christian university, there were more than a few wiseacres who decided to parody everything that came along: rules, announcements, chapel speakers...

... and songs.

One dim-bulb next door to me, J.J. by name, had an irritating habit of believing that every quip coming out of his mouth would send people into fits of hysterical laughter. None ever did. In fact, he was annoying. He'd burst into a dorm room and interrupt any conversation with a joke or a parodied song. One time he pushed open the door and was singing this very song – "He Arose" - but finished the second line with *toes* instead of *foes*. Please go back up to the stanza and see what I mean.

"Very mature, J.J.," said Rick, not looking up from the chessboard.

"And you're a college junior?" I asked.

"You like it? You guys think it's good?" asked J.J.

Wayne responded by getting up and shoving J.J. out of the room. And that was that. I never thought about that line. It was buried way back in my subconscious, never to come to the forefront. Except until now, four years later.

Remember, I wasn't reading the words in the hymn book. I was on verbal automatic pilot and coasting. And that one phrase snuck in. It came running up through the back of my head and into my mouth while I was loudly and proudly leading this song in front of a full congregation.

Yes, I said "toes." Actually, I bellowed it.

Immediately perspiration broke out under my arms. This was in the days well before YouTube, but I knew in an instant that if the word passed around that I was making a mockery of a sacred song, well, it could be brutal on my ministry, let alone shake my self-confidence beyond the point of return.

While still leading the singing, I looked about the room quickly to see if anyone actually heard my devastating musical faux pas. Only my teen sister Kandy registered any kind of response. Her eyes widened a bit, but other than that, nobody showed any surprise.

The only thing I knew was to forge on ahead as if nothing happened, and hope for the best. I pounded out the next verse with incredible dynamics, swinging my arms and encouraging the troops. I was manic now, flailing away with my arms like a zoo monkey entertaining the crowds. We finished singing and I immediately went into the message from the book of Revelation. I mean, *immediately.* I was noticing some raised eyebrows and I wanted to get to the Word before my self-confidence was shattered.

God was merciful. Nobody said a word about it. Well, at least not to me.

That next day I asked Kandy if she had heard my mistake.

"Well, of course. I mean, you just about shouted it," she said. "But the thing was, I kept telling myself that I might have misunderstood what you sang, because you kept on going as if nothing was wrong. I think that's how we all felt."

I dodged a bullet, I'm almost sure.

There's only one thing that keeps the doubt in my mind. About three years later I met Pastor Johnston at a Bible conference where we were both on the speaking schedule. I happened to meet up with him on the hotel elevator and we exchanged pleasantries as we headed to his floor. As the door opened I asked him if he was ready to speak the next day.

"Yes, but I need a bit of rest," he said as he stepped off and turned around. "I'm a bit weary from doing so much walking today."

"Really? Lot of fatigue?" I asked.

"Yes," he answered with a wink as the elevator door was closing. "Especially in my toes."

3.

Minnesota: Racing the Clock, Sobbing in the Pulpit, and Learning to Shut Up So God Can Work

It was very late and I was exhausted.

The elderly gentleman adjusted his glasses and motioned for me to sit down to a chicken salad sandwich and a coffee in the small homey kitchen.

"Please come and rest, young man," he said, gesturing with his arm. "Here. Have something to eat."

His wife shuffled over to him, holding her empty tea cup. "Now, don't you stay up too late, Ed," she said quietly. "You know how you like to go on talking." He smiled and gripped her hand as she patted my shoulder and headed for the bedroom.

Their names were Ed and Norma Phillips. They knew that they had a special ministry to me that night. I knew they did, too. It was already past eleven o'clock and I had just come in from the evening's service.

I had finished speaking at their church in Elmore, Minnesota, and as I loosened my tie, pulled the chair to the kitchen table and reached for the thick chicken salad sandwich, I was still trying to find my voice. The past few hours held a memory that would forever burn in my heart ... in *all* of our hearts, for that matter.

Mr. Phillips smiled at me. "Have you recovered yet?" he asked gently.

I returned the smile. "Yes, sir, I guess so. That... that was some kind of service we had, wasn't it?"

I thought back to how it all came about.

Like the start of numerous other days for me, things were a bit frantic as I raced across Minnesota to speak at a meeting in a small church outside of this little place called Elmore. Most of my stress was due to my self-inflicted transportation rookie mistake – I'd made a schedule of speaking engagements that were too far apart, mainly because I had wrongly estimated travel times between locations. In this case, I had driven over four hundred miles to get here, stopping only for fuel and a cup of metallic-tasting McDonald's coffee. I'd been sweating out the whole trip, arriving before the service with just under an hour's leeway. I hadn't slept since leaving a meeting in South Dakota and once again I was cutting it too close, I realized. I wasn't sure how to rectify that scheduling challenge, because I'd pretty much painted myself into a corner as far as the year's calendar – the idea of cancelling any meetings was unthinkable to me. I was going to make the best of it, but it was playing havoc with my sleep schedule.

It's not that the trip itself was rough – in fact, the traveling was, though high-speed, actually quite enjoyable. God had given me safety on the road and a great afternoon of viewing the delightful Minnesota landscape. It was my first time in the state and I was elated at the scenery: the lavender roadside wildflowers, the rustic farms with sturdy silos and wide barns, a sky that seemed to go on forever. The panorama of northern nature made the long trip seem like I was watching a travelogue. When I stopped for gas, I even sampled some local cheeses. Quite tasty indeed.

It wasn't all sightseeing, though. I was trying to make every minute count, so the Aspen became my private study. While racing along the road I had looked over my notes and prayed about the message I would give in the evening service. I had a list of topics or passages from which I had selected, but I was writing a whole new sermon as I drove. I had an odd habit during my first year on the highway circuit, and it was a habit that was as exhausting as my long-range travels: I never repeated the same message's notes - ever. I felt that if I would use the same sermon notes even twice, I would end up getting into a rut, merely repeating words that weren't fresh. That's how I felt, and I stuck to this conviction for at least one circuit around the country. Although the subject matter might be the same, each message was different due to my lack of understanding that a full-time evangelist could have a rotating file of messages and speak based upon the subjects God led him to address. At the time, my naïve reasoning was that I was cheating the congregation if I used a "recycled" sermon, so each of my messages was thrown out after I spoke. I started from scratch for the next message, even if I was speaking multiple times a day. It wasn't until late in my second year of travel that I accepted that it was no sin to file away messages for future use. It was a solution that greatly eased the stress of having to come up with new sermons constantly, as I was then preaching two or three times a day.

On this warm Minnesota afternoon I was driving with the windows open and a Bible propped on my lap, both reading the road map and studying a concordance as I went down the highway. I felt good about the subject material. For Sunday night I had settled on a message about servanthood, using a passage in the twentieth chapter in Matthew as my key text. I leaned over and used a battered "Ohio, the Buckeye State" ballpoint pen to scratch down a jostled outline while I tried to keep my eye on the road. I had plenty of time to mull over each part of the Scripture I was to use. I actually found that traveling alone in a car across vast expanses of highway is really a great way to study. The distractions were few. Since I had no radio, there was no temptation to turn on a station. I found that the only real distractions were (1) remembering not to drift into the lane of an 18-wheeler, and (2) billboards. For a person like me who battles Attention Deficit Disorder, highway billboards are like fireworks on the Fourth - try as you might to ignore them, the colorful spectacle will draw your eyes eventually. The easiest place to avoid billboard distractions was Virginia – I think they have a state law against such signage, because I don't remember seeing a single billboard along the Interstate. As far as distractions caused by an overabundance of highway advertising, it's a tie between South Carolina ("South of the Border" signs every mile) and South Dakota ("Wall Drug" signs every twenty feet).

I jotted out a few more notes and folded my paper, tucking it into the Bible on the passenger seat as I drove along Highway 169 toward the cozy town of Elmore. I felt I was ready.

Elmore's a comfortable little place with a nice park, a museum and a population of around seven hundred people. The streets are wide and the folks are openly friendly, as evidenced when I pulled up next to the church located just outside of town. If Pastor Vincent was at all concerned at how close I came to the service time, he never showed it as he greeted me warmly and allowed me some time to wash up in the next-door parsonage prior to the service, where I scrubbed some of the grit off of my face and changed my clothes. I chatted with Mrs. Vincent over coffee, and then the pastor and I spent some time in his study in prayer for that night's meeting. His was an earnest prayer of an open and honest calling to the Lord for His blessing upon the service. At any church on my circuit, the prayer times with the pastor were always especially powerful to me.

By the time we headed to the main auditorium, the service had started and the singing was well underway. Pastor Vincent escorted me to the front and bade me sit up on the platform and face the congregation. This was the only unpleasant part of the whole evening, because sitting up on the platform, to tell you the truth, was embarrassing for me, and still is to this day.

Well, as I stepped up on the platform and turned around, I was taken aback at the sight. The church was full that evening, with every pew shoulder-to-shoulder. There were even people seated in extra folding chairs in the far aisles. Perhaps they were attending out of curiosity, wanting to hear this wandering vagabond of a speaker give a presentation? Perhaps they were always faithful and packed the church every Sunday evening? I wasn't sure, but as Pastor Vincent introduced me, I had the same feeling come over me as I had in every one of the services I attended:

These people prepared themselves physically, mentally and spiritually for the meaningful Word that God would bring through a messenger. I was that messenger for the night, and I had better do a good job.

I stepped forward, opened my Bible to Matthew and looked at my notes for the introduction.

I smiled at the people and they smiled back.

"I want to thank you for allowing me to come to your church and speak," I said, and I meant every word of it. "I'm humbled when I realize that I carry the burden of handling God's Word for this congregation tonight."

I kept my gaze steady. "You could have had a number of other people in this pulpit who could do a much better job of delivering a message, but you allowed me to come. I am honored by this, and I will do my best to live up to your expectation of delivering God's Word in an effective way tonight. Would you please turn to the twentieth chapter of Matthew?"

As the people leafed through their Bible's pages and found the proper chapter, I looked down at my notes, glancing over the opening illustration I was to give.

"May I relate a story that will help explain the truth we'll find in the Bible? I want to tell you about a camp located in Texas that's been doing a wonderful service for the community for decades. It's a Bible camp, and every year there are hundreds of teenagers who come to Christ through the ministry of those dedicated people. However, there was one summer where the ministry suffered a great tragedy." I glanced down at the paper and continued.

"It was mid-summer when an unexpected storm raged through that region of the Lone Star State, sending sheets of rain down so violently that in a matter of minutes streets and roads were overwhelmed. The ground couldn't hold the quickly-rising torrents of water, and a flash flood ensued. The storm was heading right towards the remote low-lying campsite with frightening speed, made especially dangerous by the fact that the roads and paths about of the camp were primitive and, in the case of a heavy rain, quite unstable. A wide river surrounding the camp had the likelihood of flooding its banks on up to the bridge itself."

"This little Bible camp received a panicked warning both on phone and over the radio, telling them that their low-lying property was going to receive treacherous flooding very soon and the camp needed to evacuate immediately. The whole camp jumped into action, with the staff members clearing the grounds as fast as they could. The counselors piled the campers on the church bus and within minutes pulled away toward higher ground, but the bus had to cross that bridge that crossed the rapidly-rising river."

I looked across the auditorium. "Every bus made it across except for the last one. The final bus stalled as the water got to it. Kids were in danger, and a human chain of adults and older teens was formed up along the bridge and to the bus in order to pass the children to higher ground and safety. However, one boy named Steven had both legs in casts. He was on crutches and could not walk along the line of people who could help him up to the bank for safety. The water was now waist deep and still rising. "

I paused.

"William, a teenage boy of seventeen, made a decision in an instant. He grabbed Steven through the back door of the bus and hefted him high as he sloshed through the chest-deep water toward the nearest tree he could find. William shoved him up on the highest branch he could, safely above the flood waters. The campers on the bank cheered. Steven clung to the branch and smiled in relief. He looked down to thank William..."

I shuffled my notes.

"... but William was gone. The waters had swept him away. William died, giving his life for another person who couldn't save himself."

I looked down.

A tear splattered on my notes.

I looked up and choked. "This sacrifice..."

I let out a sob, despite myself. Inwardly, I was shocked.

The emotion of the story had overcome me. I wiped away a tear and tried to speak, but nothing would come. I sobbed again.

I've got to get control of my emotions.

"William made a decision..."

Tears were streaming down my face.

Dear Lord, what can I do? I couldn't continue. Besides being overcome with sadness, I now added panic to the situation. The room was packed. I was only one minute into the message. And I was, literally, speechless.

"I...uh..." I was choking back sobs, helpless while standing before scores of people. And I didn't know what to do. The room was absolutely quiet except for my strangled sobs, and people's eyes were wide open.

I've traveled all this way and I've let these people down. And I've let you down, Lord.

Then in the midst of the stillness, someone moved.

A tall blonde-haired teenage boy stood up and quietly made his way past people along the pew to the center of the aisle. He looked me right in the eye, walked toward the front and fell to his knees in prayer.

Then a middle-aged woman with a housecoat rose from the back and stepped out. She lowered her eyes and came forward, silently motioning for the pastor's wife to talk to her. They quietly kneeled off to the side.

A young husband and wife on the second row stood up and came around to an empty place on the front pew, holding hands. They knelt in prayer.

I looked on helplessly. I was still crying, struggling to regain my composure but unable to speak. As I looked from my right to my left, people were slowly coming forward in twos and threes. An elderly man walked over to the pastor and clutched his arm. They both bowed their heads in prayer. Two men at the back of the auditorium met each other, shook hands and started weeping quietly, hugging and praying. Were they making amends over a previous argument? I didn't know.

I didn't know why *any* of them were coming forward.

I looked down in front of the altar before me. There were at least thirty people kneeling and praying; some in groups, others individually. There was no music to heighten the emotions of the moment. I looked for the song leader and found him also on his face, praying near the front. There would be no music.

There didn't need to be.

More came forward. The youth pastor and his wife were praying with a group of teens over by the window near the entrance. An older couple held hands and prayed with a younger couple. Still more came. The pews were emptying.

It went on for hours, a deeply moving long-to-be-remembered service.

And now I sat in the rural kitchen of the elderly gentleman as he watched me toy with a chicken salad sandwich and stir my coffee.

"Are you embarrassed by what happened to you tonight?" he asked.

"Yes," I said. "And no." I looked up at him. "I believe my greatest emotion is shock. Perhaps awe."

49

He looked deep into his empty cup. "You realize what happened?"

"Again, yes and no, Mr. Phillips."

"Please call me Ed."

"Okay... er, Ed." I pushed the sandwich to the side. "I saw the Spirit of God move in a great way tonight. I also saw that I was personally shut down, taken out, closed up ... for reasons I don't know."

Ed Phillips put his cup down and leaned back. "Would you mind hearing a story from an old man? It may help you decipher some."

"No, sir, I don't mind at all," I said, sipping the coffee and fixing my gaze on him. He had given me a look that he was digging into his memory. I could tell that this would be significant.

He took a deep breath and began. "I've worked in construction for over two decades now. I'm the owner of my own construction company, now going on, let's see, twenty-three years. And, young man, that company is my mission field." He looked at me. "Every one of my employees is like a son to me, and I reach out with the message of Christ to each man on the job in as loving and clear way as I can. I look for opportunities."

He rose to refill his cup. "I came to Jesus while I was on the job myself, before I owned this business. It was when I was in my thirties that I was a truck driver through these parts, going to every corner of the state and hauling for one of the major companies in Minnesota. I had plenty of miles to cover, and I listened to the radio – especially talk radio – as much as possible. It helped pass the time, and gave me something to think about, as well."

He poured his cup full and walked over to fill mine. "One day I experienced some electronic interference on the radio. Must've been a storm passing through the area or something that knocked out the station that I usually listened to each afternoon. Bunch of static, you know. I was on a long stretch of road, and wanted to hear something, so I fiddled around the dial until I heard something new - unique to me, really. There was this Christian preacher talking about Jesus Christ and the road to Heaven."

He sat down. "I was so stunned by this message that I turned it on full volume. This preacher went on clear as day and in a no-nonsense way, too. I never heard this before. Man, I took in every word about God's plan of salvation, and I was desperate to know how to get this gift. Well, the preacher said it's best to get on your knees and ask Jesus in payer, so you know what I did?"

I smiled and shrugged. "I couldn't guess, sir."

He chuckled. "I pulled over to the side of the highway, got out of the truck cab, and got on my knees in the shoulder's gravel. If that was the way to ask Jesus for permission to get to Heaven, then that's what I wanted to do." He laughed aloud. "I can only imagine what the drivers along that interstate were thinking when they saw a man kneeling and praying in front of the grill of his truck."

I had to laugh aloud as well. The sight would have been priceless.

Ed Phillips raised a finger. "Three years later I started my own construction company and used each opportunity to tell my employees about Jesus Christ. A few of them were serious as they listened. But I suspected some of them were merely giving me polite attention only because I wrote the checks."

"Then one day we were digging a deep ditch for a water line. This trench was about ten feet deep, about four feet wide, and we'd dug about thirty feet in length. Before we ended the day's work, I had the workers hop out of the trench. I directed the foreman to move the arm of the digger – some folks call it the excavator – to one side so I could drop down and make an inspection before we put in the pipes the next day."

"I wasn't in the depth of that trench for twenty seconds when the whole thing collapsed on me. I was buried alive under ten feet of earth."

"I was smothered instantly, and the force of the collapse broke some of my bones, including one rib that punctured my spleen. Mainly, though, I was unable to breathe."

I shuddered. He continued.

"The boys told me later on what was going on above. The very second the section collapsed the boys leaped on the mound and clawed away with everything they had: shovels, boards, hands, anything. They were screaming and digging, because they knew they had only seconds to act and they weren't exactly sure where my head was. They knew they were going too slow. In desperation, the foreman leaped up on the digger and swung the arm out over the general area where I was and dug the claw deep into the dirt pile."

"He could've killed you," I said.

"Yes, he knew that, but he also knew I would die soon anyway, so he needed to take the risk," said Mr. Phillips. "That digging bucket came close; so close that it actually had my arm in its teeth and it ripped it from my body." He pulled back his sleeve and showed me a nauseating scar. "Only a shred of skin and muscle was holding my arm to my body."

"The hole he created gave me enough air and with the boys all digging around, they were able to get me out to safety. They put me on the stretcher and I looked up at those men. They thought it, and I thought it, too – that I was going to die. I had a peace about it, and I grasped the foreman's hand and nodded to him, nodded to every one of those boys I could see. It was going to be all right. I knew my destination if I left this life." He added some milk to his coffee and looked at the kitchen window. It had started raining and large drops were spattering on the glass, running down in smooth, crooked lines.

"I was in the hospital for two and a half months, in recuperation for almost a year after that, my arm mending and my collarbone and leg bones healing."

"And you know what?"

"Those men – every one of them – came in to visit me like clockwork. Nobody forced them to do it, no sir. They did it on their own free will. For a week I couldn't speak to them – the drugs and the trauma rendered me ineffective. But here's the thing, young man. Here's the thing." He pushed his cup aside and put his elbows on the table.

"Three of those men came to Christ that week, right in that hospital room – in front of me - while I was unable to speak. I could hear them and I could see them make that most important decision, but I couldn't do any talking. Each of those men – Barry, Scott, Jeremiah - all told me they remembered what I had said and they saw during the accident that I meant it."

"But I believe, Brad, that God was able to move when I was unable to speak." He chuckled. "I think it was like God saying, 'okay, Ed, you've done enough talking. It's time to hush up and let Me do My work.' That's what he did to reach those boys." He looked at me. "And that's what He did with you tonight. God reaches people in ways that are beyond words – that might be a harder lesson for you, since your ministry is based around words and sentences and paragraphs. It's a fine gift to be able to speak; it's just as fine a gift to learn just when to stop speaking. I remember an old preacher that came through this area saying something that applies to your situation. It was a short little prayer that went like this:

Lord, fill my mouth with worthwhile stuff;

And nudge me when I've said enough.

I watched as Ed turned and looked at the window again, studying the raindrop patterns on the window of that rural Minnesota kitchen. As I watched him I knew that I was looking at the profile of a truly great man of God.

4.

Virginia – Favorite Truck Stops, an Unlikely Convention, and the Top Hero

As the weeks rolled by, I was slowly becoming intimately acquainted with our country's Interstate system, north and south. I was also starting to get quite familiar with a number of state and county routes across the country. In fact, life on the road was like going back to college. I was taking classes ranging from *Introduction to Best Gas Prices* to *Broken Alternator 101* (I took that class twice).

My classes also extended to *Relying on God Daily 101* as well.

I was now four months into my circuit riding, and it was becoming evident that I was receiving God's clear direction to keep going. On certain occasions I would receive a firm handshake with some dollars stuffed inside. Other times I would find that my tank had been filled. Sometimes I would open my car door and see a few dollars tucked in the ashtray that was now holding all my nickels and dimes and quarters. The price of regular gas in 1983 was $1.24 a gallon, and every quarter I would find would help me move a few more miles down the road. There were even times that I would find my car had been washed, the oil had been changed, or my back seat held a package of homemade foodstuffs. It was rarely an overabundance, but it was always just enough to get me to the next destination.

Just enough. That's all I needed.

I was now sleeping in my car in a truck stop at least fifty percent of the time on the road. The rest of the times I slept at an Interstate rest stop. Hotels were an unattainable luxury, costing way more than I could pay and keep a good conscience. In fact, I am fairly confident that I can name the towns in which I actually *did* stay in a hotel during the entire two years: Rock Hill, South Carolina and Centennial, Colorado. That's it.

I will be mighty proud to tell you, though that, by George, I slept in some of the best rest stops that our Interstate network has to offer. Alabama's welcome center sticks out in my mind as one of the prettiest. Florida's won big points with me because they gave out free orange juice. Arizona's welcome center had striking architecture, and I believe it was Oklahoma's that had a fine wagon train sculpture that was a sight to behold.

Truck stops became the norm for me when I wanted to get a good bit of rest. I found them economical, safe and easily accessible to where my next stop would be. Not necessarily clean, mind you, but as long as I could get a nice cheeseburger and a safe restful parking spot, I didn't care if the linoleum was greasy. Plus, they had a nice large map on their walls so I could re-establish my bearings.

It was near midnight when I pulled into a Flying J at Joplin, Missouri and flopped across the front seat, ready to grab some sleep. Before I settled in for the night, I pulled out my flashlight and had a time of Bible reading, finding some peaceful meditations in the Psalms. I read about David's call to God, and in reflection I recalled his heroics through the Scriptures. David was a hero, all right.

As I stared to nod off, I thought back to my early recollection of heroes...

As a child growing up in Pennsylvania , I loved super heroes. I could list the many reasons why I liked these comic book characters.

Spiderman had a teen age mystery about him as well as a whole arsenal of funny quips and comebacks in the midst of battle as well.

The Fantastic Four members acted like a dysfunctional family, with jokes thrown in during times of stress. I could definitely relate to that.

Superman could pound anybody into the dust. Plus, he could fly.

Ah, but Batman and Robin were my absolute favorites, especially the TV series. I loved everything about them, from their insanely cool utility belts to their over-the-top dialogue. We'd cram around the living room TV set every Thursday night, waiting to hear that theme song which was and still is, in my opinion, the greatest television theme song in the history of broadcasting.

Oh, how we loved Batman. We lived in the little burg of Dallastown, and every kid in the elementary school loved Batman. And Robin, of course. The TV show was the talk of the school. Playground time was all Caped Crusader stuff.

As a kid, I wanted to be a superhero. I wanted to take on bad guys and send 'em to the hoosegow. I wanted to fly. I wanted to run faster than a car or train, for that matter. I wanted to team up with other powerful beings and form a league like the Avengers or the Justice League of America. I was totally, dead serious. That's no big secret; virtually every boy in America wants to be a super hero.

But unlike other kids, I had a secret on how to make it actually happen. I wasn't going to just *dream* about it, doggone it, I was going to *do* something about it.

And I've kept a secret about my background with superheroes until now. I am going to tell you the absolute truth. This one is going to be hard for anyone to swallow, but I swear it is true, down to every detail.

I was so serious that I actually tried to organize a superhero convention. In real life.

I was going to hold an international super hero convention in Dallastown, Pennsylvania.

I was in second grade at the time.

It's true.

As a second grader, I was so serious about gathering the Good Forces of the World that I flopped down on the floor of my bedroom (actually, I shared the room with two of my brothers at the time) and got to work on an undercover project. I hauled out my crayons and a piece of cardboard (cut painstakingly from the side of a refrigerator box), made a large poster and marched downtown in order to recruit superheroes to help me organize a league of do-gooders. It was time for action, and I was making the first move.

Remember, these were the dynamic TV years of the George Reeves Superman, Green Hornet (with Bruce Lee as Kato), and as I had said, my personal Mt. Everest of all crusaders: Batman. There were plenty of superheroes to go around, so why couldn't I organize some of them? I'd watch the television, wishing that I could team up with these guys, and wonder of wonders I noticed the glaring loophole (at least on television) that none of them seem to buddy up with each other as allies against evil - or even a good laugh at a backyard barbecue, for that matter.

Fueling this insane idea was my dad's purchase of two crates - *crates*, mind you – jammed with comic books ranging from early Iron Man, Spiderman, Aqua Man (I didn't really like him), Silver Surfer, Hulk, and others.

You could see I was a mess.

I would sit and read the old DC and Marvel comics and just hope against hope that I could be a superhero. We would, of course, gather into neighborhood superhero groups of our own in the gravel lot near our home with our own custom-made names and powers: FleetFoot, Inferno, Ultra Boy, Invisible Girl and even Glasses Man (That was my name. I found an old pair of plastic glasses with no lenses and figured they were good for laser beams. I was short on creativity that day, *okay?* That persona lasted for one week before I threw it away in disgust.). My dad supplied a set of old capes from a defunct high school band drum major corps, and we were set. Every day - and I do mean *every day* - we were running the lawns of the little town, defying imaginary hoodlums who all wore pork-pie hats and masks. I never could figure out why they would stereotype themselves that way, but that was their business, not mine.

But back to the convention.

I wanted to take it step further. I *knew* the world superheroes lurking around, just waiting to get organized. They just needed a leader. And I, a knowledgeable second grader, would be the one to band them together...and the International Headquarters would be in Dallastown, Pennsylvania... and I was absolutely serious about all this.

I truly believed that I could call the great heroes of the universe together and organize an ad-hoc Justice league of my own. Think of it! We could protect the world from all of the ills of the 60's... *if we could just get organized.* And I, a second grader from Dallastown Elementary, would be the one to bring them together.

Why I believed that the titans of the world would gather and obey my instructions, I cannot tell you. I just figured that they, being fair and kind much like they were in the comic books, would allow me to be President-Elect or Headquarters guy or something. How I was supposed to know where the immediate crimes were? I hadn't figured that out either - the first thing was to get organized, for crying out loud.

So I took that crayon-covered hunk of cardboard that was about 3 feet square and walked downtown. It said this:

ATTENTION SUPER HEROES

of any powers. All are welcome.

TIME TO ORGANIZE.

Meet at Dallastown Park

at home plate today at 3 p.m.

ALL SUPER HEROES WELCOME.

I walked down to Glatfelter's Furniture and was going to ask them to put it in their window, but when I got in the store, heard their in-store elevator-type music and saw the finery, I realized that they might not understand my quest. I got cold feet and backed out of the door, a bit unnerved. I went outside and stood on the downtown sidewalk, figuring out my plan.

Ah. A superhero wouldn't care if the poster was on the inside of a store or on the street, would he? Of course not! They all have an inner-distress signal anyway, telling them someone needed them. *They just had to tune in to their personal distress frequency and they'd be directed to this sign.* I propped the brown cardboard sign in front of the store on the sidewalk and took off running. Nobody should know it was me who put the sign there. All things must be secret, you understand.

I went to the park and hung back throughout the afternoon - not wanting to give away my secret identity. That, plus the risk of getting yelled at by an old guy sitting near the monkey bars. I waited. 2:45 p.m. came and I was in a sweat. This was going to be good.

2:55.

2:59.

They'll all fly in, at the last minute.

3 p.m.

Man, these guys aren't very punctual. Still, they have floods and fires to take care of...

Ten minutes went by and nobody showed up.

Ten more minutes...

... at 3:30 p.m. I walked back to Charles Street and went to my room, deeply disappointed and yet a bit relieved as well. During my wait I realized that I wasn't sure what to do if a whole mob of heroes with assorted powers showed up.

I sat in that Flying J parking lot and laughed out loud. What a strange kid I was. I would have liked to have seen the reaction of the employee who found the sign in front of their store later that evening at closing time.

Now here I was, years later, still admiring heroes. But a different set of heroes.

I was truly seeing the grassroots Christian of America face-to-face on the ground level of life. I wasn't glad-handing spiritual celebrities who were onstage in front of footlights – I was out where the Believer rolled up his or her sleeves and got their fingernails dirty: at home, in the office, on the farm, in the church – all sorts of common places.

And I was meeting uncommon people. Uncommonly *good* people.

I thought of George, a West Virginia preacher who held a second job in order to be able to serve his church congregation of three families for over ten years. He also worked to help keep a farm available for a Bible camp whenever there was a need –complete with bathroom facilities and pavilion.

I thought of Mike, the Oklahoma mechanic who went out of his way on a rush-hour Friday to assist me along the Interstate when my tire shredded beyond repair due to a shard of metal on the road. When he discovered – to my great embarrassment - that my spare would not hold air, he reached in the back of his truck and pulled out a brand new tire and mounted it. Before I knew it he was pulling back on to the freeway and waving to me, refusing any kind of payment for his generous services.

I think of Willie, the kindly bachelor gentleman suffering from a severe birth defect that cost him most of the use of his arms. He was an unpaid Michigan youth pastor of a miniscule youth group - four youngsters. With no fanfare or hoopla, this fifty-something gentleman had been quietly paying for all his teen group's expenses, including all mission trips and Christian camp tuition. He was also actively mentoring, a lost art in many churches.

Then there was Pearl, the portly and jovial grandmother who lived in a clapboard home with peeling paint and five – count 'em – *five* junked cars in the driveway. She and her husband were barely making ends meet, yet she packed me with a box of Tupperware filled with beans, chicken, stews, biscuits and cookies whenever I came through southern Georgia to speak at her church. Like the great woman of Shunem who built a room for the traveling Elisha, this woman had her husband construct a private room for me so that I could have a comfortable bed whenever I passed through the area.

Heroes, all of them.

It was great to get to share God's blessing by teaching in the many venues, but as the months went by I was learning as much as I was teaching. It's just as great, I must say, to be on the receiving end of a blessing that you can clearly see could only come from God. Every day was like going to a special interactive classroom, and I was getting a cross-country education. Some of them still bring a deep emotion back to me.

In Norfolk, Virginia, I spent over two hours with a pastor whose time in Korea had netted him a leg injury that had plagued him ever since. He was crippled but he had no complaints whatsoever. This gentle soul sat and shared the near-death experiences he faced while under mortar attack while in the military, dodging explosions and being successful in escaping them... well, all but one. In the middle of the restaurant he rolled up his pant leg and showed me the hideous purple scar running from his ankle up to his high. But telling war stories wasn't the reason he spent so much time with me; he was heartbroken for the college-age young people of the Chesapeake region. We sat over coffee and he prayed with me for new horizons that I might find in reaching young people for Christ. Just before I got in the car, he stuffed a handful of dollars in my hand, enough to get me to my next church with a bit of Burger King money to spare.

In Rocky Mount, North Carolina, a group of deacons stood in the parking lot of a barbecue shack late one night and laid hands on my head while openly (even loudly) calling to the Lord to sustain me in my travels and to give me peace in the times of trouble that I might face on the road. And keep my car in one piece. I became emotional as I felt those blessings of fervent prayers for my safety, both physically and spiritually. As I pulled out I saw that someone had laid an envelope of money with enough to get me to my next stop across the state. Oh, and there was also a barbecue burger wrapped up neatly, next to the envelope.

In Mesa, Arizona, I was encouraged, humbled and truly enthralled as a group of adults sat for hours giving testimonies. They were humble in telling of their walks with Christ and the many witnessing opportunities they had in sharing the love of Jesus with their neighbors and co-workers. While I sat and listened to them, some of the church members snuck out with my keys and took my car to the local car wash – as well as a nearby dealership.

When I got into my car I discovered that my little Dodge Aspen had undergone a full tune-up as well as a lube, oil and filter change.

Other blessings came my way. I spoke at a chapel service at a school in Glendale, Arizona to a small school, squeezed into a tight schedule due to the school's Picture Day. I had fifteen minutes to speak. In fifteen minutes, eleven students came forward to accept Christ as their Savior. One by on they lined outside the makeshift counseling room, and I was able to talk with each one of them personally about their decision. Man, that's priceless.

What memories.

I shifted my head on the car's armrest and thought about the Christian heroes that the Lord was introducing to me all along the circuit.

Up to this point in my travels, which hero was the most impressive to me?

That would take me back to a one-day stop that I made in western Virginia. I had finished a series of meetings in Norfolk and was due the next week at a camp in Bucyrus, Ohio, so I had sprinkled meetings along the route as I made my way north. As I had said, a number of tiny schools and assemblies were happy to let me minister to them once they realized that there were no travel expenses involved. I had contacted the leader months before and let him or her know the day and date that I would literally be cruising by their front door. To a tiny assembly, organization, mission, or school with little or no budget for speakers, few things were as advantageous as having a speaker who didn't ask for gas money or even set a fee for speaking. If the hat passed was nothing but a handful of quarters, I was happy to take that. I started finding that there were scores of Christian schools who yearned for speakers outside their region but due to costs could only request local pastors. While having a neighboring minister as a guest speaker was often a wonderful experience in itself, I met many principals who were quite happy for a "change of pace" - to have someone from outside their locality.

I remember that I was to speak in chapel at a small school near Roanoke whose school year was finishing in late June, a not uncommon thing in the 1980 decade. The school was in its early growth stages, with most of the classes being held in the dimly-lit unpainted basement of the church. I didn't hear any complaints from the kids, though, and was delighted with the upbeat atmosphere. In fact, *the students had invented their own dress code.*

The girls and guys voted on it unanimously, and as I walked in I was greeted with the best-dressed student body I'd ever seen: every boy was wearing a dress shirt and tie with no tennis shoes or sneakers allowed, while each girl wore either a skirt or dress. Like I said, this was the student body's choice – the only time I had ever encountered this.

I was also encouraged by the openness of the chapel time, for the student body was quite receptive. While I tried to avoid anecdotes or superfluous travelogue stories, the principal insisted that after my Bible message, I share some stories of life "on the road." She was eager to let the students hear about the here-and-now adventures of a missionary. It took me aback; I had never been called a missionary, but she made it clear to the kids – and to me – that mission work within American borders was much needed.

After the chapel finished and the students headed back to class, I was pulled aside by the principal.

"Brad, would you mind speaking to a young girl? She really needs to talk to you, and she asked specifically for you."

I was ushered into a small side room and sat down across the table from a petite dark-haired girl of about thirteen years of age. Her name was Donna, and she held a Kleenex box. She was silently weeping.

"Mister Brad, I need your help," she said.

"How can I help you, Donna?" I asked.

"I need to learn how to pray about a situation," she responded, pulling out a tissue and wiping her nose. "A very serious situation."

She paused, gathering her thoughts.

"Every day I walk to school and back, the distance of about two miles each way," she said, blinking. "That's where the trouble is. When I'm about a half a mile from my home every afternoon, there is a boy - Randy's his name - who comes out and starts following me. I knew him years back when we both went to elementary school across town. Then he moved to another school and I didn't see him for a few years. He was a real nice boy, and friendly, too."

She fingered the box. "Then we both went to the same middle school, a public school. In fact, we had most of our classes together. Randy was still really nice, and when I started going to church and became a Christian, he visited my youth group a few times and made some friends. Everyone seemed to like Randy, 'cause he was funny and really talkative in a good way."

She waved her hand. "Our school is fairly new. When the church first announced that they were going to start this school, my parents and I knew that I would sign up to go, and I enrolled – so did a few of my friends from church. But Randy didn't ... it wasn't because of anything bad, it's just because his folks didn't see that it was necessary for him. Something like that."

Donna shifted in her seat. "Well, I don't know about when his school classes are over each day, but from the first day I started walking to school, he'd come down off the steps of his house and start following me. He wouldn't walk beside me at first – he'd walk a few steps back. Then after about a block, he'd start edging up alongside of me. It's like he was getting up his nerve or something. He still does it, even this morning. First coming up behind me and then moving alongside me..." She paused.

I waited.

"...and he starts talking filthy. He wants me to ... well... he wants me to do things with him. He talks trashy. Real pornographic stuff." She squeezed her eyes and started crying.

"Then he'll start mocking me. He'll make fun of my talk, my intelligence, even my body ..."

I was shaken. "How long has this been going on?"

"All year, every school day," she said, fighting the sobs. "Twice a day."

"Have you talked with the school about your safety? Your parents? The police?"

"Well, no," said Donna, twisting the Kleenex.

"Why not?"

"Because he's so wrong in what he's doing..." she said, but she flopped her hands in frustration. "Well, what I mean is, I'm not crying because I'm scared of him or that I'll get tempted..."

She looked at me. "*He needs Jesus.* I'm *so* burdened for his soul that it crushes me. Each day when he walks alongside me, I realized that" – she punched the table with her finger at every word – "*I'm walking beside a boy who's not going to Heaven.* Sure, he talks big and he talks filthy, but he's a guy who's going to end up in tragedy forever ... and that's more than I can handle."

The tears started flowing freely now. "In fact, when he starts talking like that, I'll talk to him about Jesus, but he'll try to ignore it. I try so hard to tell him about the Bible, so hard..." She looked in my eyes. "Mister Brad, Randy needs to see Jesus' face."

Obviously, the first things we talked about were the necessary steps to take for her safety. Then we prayed for direction.

And as we did, my head – and heart – were swimming with this new revelation: a person who cared not a whit about her safety or pride. Her heart was truly broken for a lost person. This girl was actually weeping for an unsaved person ... *who was daily tormenting her.* She wanted Randy to see Jesus' face.

Ah, Donna, you're such a hero. God brought you into my life for one microscopic afternoon to learn once again about the compassion of Jesus. I go back to the early pages of the Bible and remember Jeremiah sitting on the hill overlooking the devastation of Jerusalem. He had suffered loss personally, but his heart was broken for others - those who were facing God's wrath because of their mockery and indifference.

Jesus would, centuries later, perform the same action, despite the fact that he was getting daily persecution and rebuttal. I remember Him overlooking the city while sitting on a hill and calling out the compassionate cry that "you could have been protected as a hen gathers her chicks under her wings, but you didn't want that protection... so now your house is desolate."

Donna was my hero, helping me realize that my Christian life needed to be renovated back to the foundation of the Christian servant: loving and praying for the lost so they could see Jesus for who He really was and is. Praying so that they could see Jesus' face.

Donna's humble heroics re-focused my spiritual eyesight. I was reminded that this is what my ministry should always be – to show men how to seek His face.

Psalm 11:7 "For the LORD is righteous, he loves justice; upright men *will see His face.*"

Psalm 16:11 "*In Your presence (in Your face)* is fullness of joy; In Your right hand there are pleasures forever."

Psalm 17:15 "As for me, I shall *behold Your face* in righteousness; I will be satisfied with Your likeness when I awake."

Bible scholars tell us that in the times of the Psalms, if a subject fell on his face to ask his king for a favor, the monarch would lean over and would literally raise the man's head as a sign that the request would be fulfilled. To *lift someone's face* came to mean primarily to grant a favor, and to make that person extra-special. The New Testament Greek word *prosopoleptes* ("respecter of persons") literally meant a "face-taker." This is God's promise to those who are His children and have sought His face: He will make them special to Him. It's the granting of the greatest wish of any Christian: to be with the Lord forever.

God will lift the face of the Christian, granting him favor.

He is all-powerful. He grants mercy. He shows kindness.

He's my hero.

5.

South Dakota – a Ninety-Mile Chase, Thin Sheetrock and the Miracle Of the Pickup in the Parking Lot

I was traveling across Nevada on Highway 50, with plenty of time to think. Highway 50 is known as the Loneliest Road in America, and traversing its route is one of the most serene drives I'd taken – a wide open, orange and yellow landscape bisected by a grey ribbon of road running ahead of you. The effect is surreal, and often has a hypnotizing effect on the traveler. The last time I rode this corridor I came upon a group of sandy-haired surfers with California plates who were testing out the bounce-factor of their low-rider shock absorbers while doing sixty miles per hour. I recall shaking my head and re-focusing to see if I was actually seeing different corners of the car of the Dodge Charger bob up and down like a Warner Brothers cartoon.

Four years prior to that, I had taken this very route alongside a college grad friend of mine as we both headed West to start our careers – he in his El Camino, me in my '64 Chevy Stepside pickup – and we tried to complete the entire state's journey in one night, chatting by CB radio. Things were going smoothly along Highway 50 with two exceptions: two grumpy truckers and Dave's bright headlights. Dave had the curious habit of driving at night with his high beams on, believing that it made him more conspicuous to traffic around him. Well, at three o'clock in the morning, his bright-light antics did more than make him conspicuous – it enraged two semi-tractor trailer drivers who thought he was taunting them by blinding them in their rear-view mirrors.

Listening to them on channel 19, I overheard their plans to run him off the road. I tried all kinds of things to get him to pay attention to their chatter on the CB but he had turned the volume low. By catching up alongside Dave and signaling for him to drop down to channel 5, I was able to alert him without them hearing my conversation. It didn't matter, though, because they put two and two together, figured I was driving with him and decided to target me as well.

What transpired next was out of a silent-era Keystone Kops movie. Our four vehicles were involved in an uphill-downhill chase for over ninety miles on Highway 50, with us gaining speed on the inclines and them barreling dangerously close to us on the downhill sections. Dave and I were able to stay just barely ahead of them until we lost them in downtown Carson City. We made it out alive, I'm happy to tell you. Dave and I waved good-byes at the state line and headed to start our respective careers and ministries.

As I cruised along Highway 50 I also reminisced about the previous week's events, and I had to laugh. Talk about weird situations.

Now, I've often been accused of coming up with some odd ways to find solutions, and even though the answers work for me, I discover that people view me as quite strange afterwards.

One proof was when I was a youth pastor in Tennessee. A dozen teens prepared for a summer mission trip which was to be near Alliance, Ohio where the weather was brutally hot that time of year. The church was a storefront ministry, and young pastor Brent McKamey and his wife Kate were happily starting a strong outreach in the community. The church had written me and asked me to come to hold a week of meetings and help create a children's ministry and a youth group, all within a week's time. After we arrived in Ohio, I spoke that Sunday from the book of Nehemiah about the opportunity to build and have a prayer time. We were all excited and rarin' to go.

The next day was a day of visitation for the Vacation Bible Time, which would start on Tuesday and go through Saturday.

It was brutally hot, as I had said, and the humidity was stifling. The van we were using had no air conditioning and everyone was dripping sweat and, to put it delicately, growing peculiar and pungent odors as the day wore on. We were drenched and grimy from running door-to-door, but still the youngsters kept pushing on – a dedicated bunch of troopers, every one of 'em. As we flopped down in the storefront church's main room that evening, the young pastor and his wife came in to let us know about housing arrangements.

"Boys," he said, wiping his face with a handkerchief, "you'll be staying here at the church for your sleeping quarters. Girls, my wife Kate has you all parceled out to different families, two to a home. The girls will have dinners with the host families, and the boys can eat from anything we have in the church refrigerator."

Piper raised his hand weakly. "Pastor Brent, where will we get cleaned up? The church doesn't have any baths or showers."

Kate stepped forward. "I've taken care of that, Piper. Boys, you'll go three houses down to one of our members' homes. You'll take shifts and use the shower there." She smiled. "Isn't that nice of them?"

Yes, it was nice, but we were soon going to find out that it wasn't quite effective.

We shuffled over to the brick homestead one block away and sat looking at each other while, one by one, the boys took a shower. The house was small and tidy, and parents were a quiet sort, but we discovered that their only child wasn't. The folks seemed overjoyed that we could come over to give them company but I soon realized why: they had no control over their child. While we sat and tried to make pleasant conversation and while doing our best not to sweat even more (the home had no air conditioning), little Ralph was tearing the place to shreds. He threw pillows, crayons and hot wheels cars in reckless abandon, knocked over the lamp and tore the curtains, earning merely a quiet "now, now" from the mother. Our boys were gamely trying to entertain the boy with some lighthearted interaction but Ralphie was interested in nothing less brutal than a game that involved breaking something in the vicinity. The father was quietly smiling and looking at a blank television screen, giving me the impression that he couldn't wait for us to leave so he could watch re-runs of "Gunsmoke."

As each boy took his turn and came out of the bathroom, I saw a grim look on each one's face. When it was my turn I discovered why: there was no water pressure whatsoever. Taking a shower here was like trying to stand under a melting ice cube. We were sweating more water than the showerhead was delivering.

I realized that the record-breaking humidity was causing us to lose the fight to stay clean, and as well-meaning as the good folks were, the shower pressure was not doing anything for us. After laying on sleeping bags wiping the unwashed oils off of our faces, I realized that desperate times called for desperate measures. We still smelled; I had to come up with a plan before we met the girls and the pastor for breakfast.

The next morning I woke the boys at five-thirty. "Up, guys – we need to move quickly. We're getting washed up."

"Why are we getting up so early, Brad? Their shower will still be the same way, no matter what time of day. And Ralphie will be there, too," said Tate, standing up and rubbing his head.

Piper rested on one elbow. "I feel all gritty. Can't we do something? We can't go back there to get another pseudo-shower tonight."

"Boys, gather close, but not too close," I said, and the guys obediently huddled up. "I've been thinking about this all night and this is the only solution I can think of." I looked around. "You got your swim trunks, right?"

"Sure do, Brad," said a fellow named Buck. Tate also nodded. "We all do. Why?"

I looked each one of them in the eye. "Because in ten minutes, my friends, we're all going to get the most intensive shower you've ever had in your life. Hurry, we've got to beat the traffic." The guys shifted and glanced at each other.

"What?" asked Buck. "What do you mean?"

I continued with as much authority as I could. "I mean, you don't want the main street traffic to see you taking a shower, do you? Pull on your swim trunks and head to the van. We're going to the car wash. And bring plenty of change in quarters."

I loaded up the very confused males complete with swim attire, cakes of soap and beach towels. It was now 5:40 a.m.

The boys were groggy, leaning their heads against the windows of the van. I turned onto the main thoroughfare. "Does everyone have at least two quarters?" I asked. "We need quarters."

"Yessir," said Tate. "Just like you said."

75

Buck yawned and shivered. "I had a nightmare about Ralphie."

In three miles we found a self-serve car wash along the main street. I pulled the van into the front entrance facing the highway, ahead of the bay of the car wash area. The van would block us as much as possible from any traffic going by. I still wasn't sure if this was legal.

"Okay, then," I said as confidently as possible. "Keep the towels in the van but bring the quarters, boys. Go quickly, now."

"Uh, that's gonna sting a bit, won't it?" asked Piper.

I nodded. "I guess so. Pressure from a home shower head is like 60 psi. This wand is going to be shooting out faster than 800 psi, so yeah, don't go diving into it. It could be rough, but let's face it, we're desperate."

The boys quietly nodded.

I continued. "Here's what I'll do. I'm going to be the one who holds the wand steady. You walk in and out of the spray as much as you dare. Kind of edge into it – it has a wide spray. If you want to stand on the far end and work up toward the wand to figure out how much pressure you can take, okay. This is an experiment in industrialized cleanliness, so we've got to test different phases. After the first round of quarters, Piper will take the wand on the second round and *hold it still*."

"Boys, this is something we must do. I promise I won't move the jet spray anywhere other than straight ahead. You enter and exit and clean as much as you can feel safe. I'm stationary, you're mobile." The boys nodded slowly.

As we pushed the quarters in, I yelled, "And no wise guy punches the *'wax button'* either!"

And that's what we did. The seven of us danced around and took our chances – I can guarantee you, any dirt you have on your body is instantly removed. In fact, I'm pretty sure that hose can take off a tattoo as well.

After a half an hour of dancing and dodging and watching nervously for passing traffic, we were all virtual gems of cleanliness. By the next day we had figured out to move in and out of the jet stream without losing too much skin.

The cleansing wash must've given the boys extra energy, for the week was an amazing adventure in seeing God's grace. The children's Vacation Bible Time ran each day from ten until noontime and the little ones were learning verses, playing games and winning awards. As the teens each took turns narrating epic Bible stories that closed out the meetings each day, the parents sat in the back, sipping the RC Colas we supplied and nodded their approval. They liked what they were seeing and what their children were experiencing.

My cause of concern was the Friday night youth rally. It was a one-time event, and we weren't sure if there would be anyone coming, for the response from the area teens was extremely apathetic so far. Not one had committed to be at the church grounds on Friday. Still the group kept inviting and informing all teens in the area. The pastor was very encouraging and optimistic, but I wasn't so sure.

Friday night came, and it still seemed like this was going to go completely flat. Nevertheless, we constructed the fairground-like atmosphere with balloons, signs, banners, streamers and tables of food. It was only one hour before we got underway and nobody in the neighborhood was lurking nearby. "What'll we do if only a handful show up, Brad? Like, what if only three people show up?" asked Linda, tying the volleyball net between two trees.

"Why then, we'll give those three teens the best night of their lives and realize that three was the exact number that God wants us to have to start the youth group," I replied, but inwardly I admit that I was now getting worried. Wouldn't it be strange to have thirteen of us hovering over three or four teens? The situation wouldn't look very promising if that came down to it. "Let's just stop right now and pray," I said. And we did. The meeting was to start at 7 p.m. to let the evening breezes cool down the church yard. When six-thirty came and went, I looked around and saw nobody. We kept blowing up balloons and filling Coke cups.

Lord, I'd be happy if seven showed up.

As six forty-five passed by, there wasn't a visitor anywhere to be seen. *Lord, it'd be great if four showed up.* We kept looking toward the street and didn't see a car. Still we hung up streamers and got out the volleyball.

Then at five minutes before seven, it broke loose.

We had been looking toward the street, and not one person came in. The fact was, they were all coming over the fence and squeezing between the tree branches on the back of the property.

"I count ten so far," said Linda, stepping back in amazement.

"Look over there! More are coming down that side alley!" yelled Piper.

Tate made a quick head count as the teens ran over to the volleyball court and started playing. "Forty-eight, preacher!"

That was the first meeting of what would soon become the church youth group. We soon found that virtually every teen that came was from a broken home and was looking for stability. It was the love of Jesus that had my youth group teens befriend and join up with those teens in the space of one evening. We played three games of sweltering volleyball, ran an arm-wrestling tournament and gobbled down two tables' full of hot dogs, chips, Cokes and ice cream.

The more cynical side of me figured that we'd lose at least a third of the visitors once we went inside for the message. To my surprise and delight (and shame for my lack of belief) all forty-eight teens squeezed into the church's main room for my message.

I told the story of John chapter three as simple and straightforward as I could. I told of Nicodemus' search and Jesus' no-nonsense answers. I shared the truth about the reality of both heaven and hell, and the decision that needed to be made.

"Nobody's forcing you, friends," I said in conclusion, "but I'd like to know if there would be anyone who would like to make a decision to take Jesus into their lives. Would you like to give your life over to Christ and let Him have control?" The teens held a dead-level stare at me. "Let's bow our heads for some privacy," I said, "and if anyone in here would like to make that decision - the choice to take on Jesus and become a Christian – and you'd like to talk to someone further, would you raise your hand?"

One hand went up. Two. Five. Ten.

The hands kept going up and stopped at forty.

I was stunned. "Uh, put your hands down again," I said, "but keep your heads bowed. I want to make sure that you all understand what I'm saying." I explained it again. Again, forty hands went up.

"Well, then," I said. "If you're really serious, then look up at me."

Forty heads raised and looked at me.

"I want to know that you really mean it," I said. "If you are serious about this decision for Jesus, stand up." Forty teens stood up.

"And if you want to make a decision right now, come forward to the front."

All forty teens came to the front.

What transpired that night was one of the most amazing events that ever occurred in my ministry. Forty teens sat patiently along the wall as each of our teens began to minister. The pastor and his wife joined us as the young people took time with each person in showing both boy and girl the miraculous plan of salvation. It was a moment that would be burned into each teen worker's memory. God was working in an awesome way. After the commitments to salvation, the visitors made promises to come that week for the church's very first teen meeting ever.

The next day, the pastor was addressing the whole group as I was preparing to leave. "You've made history here," he said, his voice cracking. "This ministry will never be the same after this week. Years from now you can come back here and see the fruits of your labor." We were all emotional – it was a special time.

Few things in the Christian walk can surpass the feeling of personally witnessing God's miraculous kingdom work right before them.

But as we arrived back to Tennessee, happy and victorious with the work that we had witnessed, do you know the first – and may I say the most continuous - comment we heard for the next month?

"You mean you guys actually took showers in a car wash?"

So like I said, I had been getting a reputation for getting into odd situations.

This week had been that way.

It started when I was speaking to a small group of teens in a Sunday School at a church in Maryland. The teen room was under construction, and there were still some sawhorses and paint cans tucked in the corner, so the chairs were pushed up closer to me, and the meeting had a feel of a friendly conversation. After our prayer time I spoke to the youngsters from the book of Revelation, especially in the final three chapters. As it turned out, I miscalculated how long the Sunday School time was, and I finished way too early. We had plenty of time before the main service, so the teens wished to hold a Q & A session with me about various topics, and I was agreeable to the idea. Lauren wanted to know how old my car was. Jenny asked about the most difficult audience I'd ever spoken to on the circuit. Then a fellow named Zack asked if Christian college were a good choice.

"All I can tell you, my man, is that Christian college made up some of the best years of my life," I responded.

Zack waved his had dismissively. "Yes, I know what you'll try to tell me, how the classes are Bible-oriented and all, but I already know that's what a Christian college is about. What I want to know is: can you have *fun*? What kind of stuff can you do?"

"How much time do we have?" I laughed. "Tell me when the main service starts and I'm supposed to shut up, and I'll give you a run-through of my personal experiences, so you'll know what a great time you can have from a first-hand account."

For the next ten minutes I crammed tales of playing on my beloved Chi Alpha Pi's volleyball championship team, my stint as an actor in a Shakespeare play (although I was only a walk-on), and my experience as a campus radio deejay. I also jammed in stuff about hundred-foot banana splits, wrestling tournaments, debate clubs, Christmas concerts, all-campus snowball wars, comic operas and anything else I could think of offhandedly.

"Time's up," called a red-haired fellow named Jeff. "And thanks."

"Okay, then, let's head to the main service," I said, and we grabbed our Bibles. A middle-aged lady came around the corner and pulled at my sleeve.

"Preacher, I needed you to know that my daughter and husband couldn't make it here today because of a trip out of town, but Penny is ready to head to college," she said. "We all have been praying about whether she should go to a Christian college – Penny said that since we were paying her first year of tuition, she'd go wherever we felt comfortable – but we'd been under the impression that all Christian colleges were boring, like, well, like monasteries. "

She smiled. "I was in the nursery on the other side of this wall"- she pointed to the thin unfinished sheetrock that made up a flimsy divider between the rooms – "and both babies in the nursery were sound asleep, so I contented myself with listening to what you had to say about enjoying Christian college. God put me here so that I could make up my mind. We're going to send Penny to your Christian college." And they did.

In fact, Penny stayed all four years and graduated with her B.A. from that Christian college, because of the Lord using my big mouth to transmit through some flimsy sheetrock.

Then I had a meeting in Nevada that wasn't so memorable for the meeting itself but what occurred afterwards. I was to speak for just one service, but the church was kind enough to give me a place to sleep at a host family's home that evening so I could head out to California refreshed the next morning. Pastor Bentley was a nice fellow, although quite nervous and very forgetful, as I found out. In the space of one hour he had mislaid his keys, his sunglasses and his calendar. He was enthusiastic, though, and had some great projects in mind. Throughout the main part of the day we teamed up in his office at his home across town from the church. I assisted him in setting up a fall Bible conference for young adults – lots of planning and paperwork. He openly admitted that he was extremely nervous about this very first area-wide college-age Bible conference, and he needed help. We filled up whiteboards, covered yellow legal pads and lined the wall with Post-It notes. The hours went by. He asked questions and looked for ideas, while I ran out to my car and pulled out notebooks filled with conferences and conventions that I had helped create over the previous months and years. We were working right up to the time of the evening service, which was to start at seven o'clock, when the phone rang.

"Oh, yeah, I forgot," he said into the phone. He looked over at me. "Uh, Brad, do you want to have dinner right now? It's at a home over near the town park. Steak, potato... pretty fancy stuff." He grinned.

I looked up from notebook, glancing at the clock. "You mean *now*, Pastor? We have only twenty-five minutes until the evening service starts, and you told me that we're ten minutes away from the church as it is."

He slapped his forehead. "Yeah, yeah, you're right." He covered the phone with his hand. "But it's your choice. Do you want to eat now or after the service?"

I was thrown by this. By simple math, this was impossible. Just getting to that house would take almost fifteen minutes. There was no way we could cram a steak into our mouths and make it to church on time, so I looked at him and said, "After the service, for sure."

He nodded and spoke into the phone. "No." He hung up the phone. "Wow, we gotta hurry," he said, and we ran to the car and made it to the church about two minutes late. The service went fine.

After the service, however, was another story.

An older couple in their late sixties had the home where I would be staying that night. Mr. Green was playing the role of a generous host. His wife, however, was a different story.

She had a full-out tantrum in front of me. Yes, a tantrum.

The pastor had made a grievous error. We were supposed to be at the host home for a T-bone steak dinner at 5:30 that evening, enjoying the many culinary nuances of a woman who could've had her own cooking show on television. She was more than willing to show off her skills to a traveling speaker. What happened, I later found out, was that the pastor totally botched up the times and in his absent-minded way, appeared to give her the false information that I didn't care about eating her meal at all. He, of course, was wrong.

But her response was one for the books.

While Mr. Green sat at the dinner table and tried to make light conversation that evening, Mrs. Green slammed pantry doors

and crashed dishes to the counter. She threw silverware down
on the table with a *clang* so hard, so help me, it bounced in front
of me.

She threw the entire steak meal away (as a punishment to me, I
suppose) and slammed together some chicken salad sandwiches.

Mr. Green was fighting a losing battle on etiquette, but bless
him, he was still in there trying. "Well, what have we here?" he
said, looking at the two-inch high sandwiches that she *thunked* in
front of us. Indeed, they *were* fantastic-looking.

"If you don't like it, *don't eat it*," she snapped. She spun on her
heel and announced, "I'm going to bed. Get your own drinks."
She slammed the door.

The next morning the pastor's wife called and straightened out
the messy situation, with the pastor coming over personally to
apologize. Mrs. Green was mortified at her behavior and begged
forgiveness. All was well with the world as I puttered out of
Nevada with a tangible evidence of a truce pact: a whole apple
pie.

Oh, yeah, it was easy to forgive.

The odd situations continued through the week. I spent a few
days in central California speaking in San Francisco where the
conclusion of the church service struck me with curiosity.

As I was drawing the message to a close, I noticed three people –
two men and a woman – who had been disruptive throughout
my message and were bringing their rebellious attitude to a peak.
They had been exercising numerous facial expressions during
the service, openly trying to let me know that they not only
hated the message, they hated me. I mean it when I say they
were not merely annoyed, but were trying to show open
hostility toward every sentence I spoke. Aside from out-and-out

screaming profanities across the auditorium, they did everything possible to show an abhorrence to the entire service. They grimaced, rolled their eyes, shook their heads, even clenched their teeth and glared. I was surprised that they didn't regale me with, well, "hand signals" during the message.

When I asked for a time of concluding prayer, they simply glared at me and sneered.

To be honest, I was not so much intimidated as I was curious. *Why would they come to a service?* Was their purpose to disrupt, and if it was, why didn't they? There was nobody immediately next to them – had they come of their own volition?

I made it a point to head toward them and greet them before they left the auditorium. When they saw me coming they quickly moved to the side door and were gone. Okay, so they didn't want a confrontation, either.

After the congregation filed out for the morning and Pastor Levitz was locking up, I asked him about the Angry Trio.

"Curious story," he said, "and one that carries a lesson."

He sat down on a nearby chair. "About ten months ago at the conclusion of a service, these three people approached me and asked if I might be able to give them two hundred dollars for them to get a hotel room for the night. They also asked about getting another fifty dollars for some food because they claimed that they hadn't eaten in two days. Their drive shaft was in need of repair, they claimed, and they wanted a place to stay since it seemed as if their transportation would be gone."

"I looked at the three of them and said, 'You don't recognize me, do you?' They stared at me blankly. 'You came in here three weeks ago with the very same story, asking for the exact amounts of money. In fact, a ministerial friend of mine said that you came to *his* church last week with the very same story.' They turned pale. They'd been found out. I said quietly, 'I'm going to ask you to leave, right now.'"

Pastor Levitz looked up at me. "Even though I was trying to be discreet, a sixty-year old lady in our church had moved over toward us and overheard this exchange. When she heard my comments, she was so filled with what you might call 'righteous indignation' that she started reaming me out. 'How dare you talk to these people that way, Pastor!'"

"'Ma'am,' I replied, 'you're not aware of what these people are doing around the city. They're con artists who are abusing the compassion of good people.' She lit into me. 'Have you no compassion? And you're supposed to be a Christian!' She turned to the three of them and said, 'You can stay at my home for as long as you wish until you get back on your feet again, even if it's two weeks. As long as you come to church with me, I want you to have use of my home.' One of our deacons who stood nearby was a city policeman in uniform – he was about to go on patrol - and they glanced over at him before they shook their heads. I guess they thought that as long as they kept their part of this verbal agreement, they would be in the clear."

He shrugged. "As I said, Brad, that was ten months ago. In that time, those three have taken over this lady's house. The place reeks of marijuana and unwashed clothes. Junk food wrappers are everywhere. They've trashed the living room and they're up all hours of the night. None of them have jobs – they're living off of her Social Security income."

"Why doesn't she kick them out?" I asked.

"She's petrified of them," Pastor Levitz answered, standing up. "She's now asked me to throw them out, but obviously I have no legal standing to do so. The policeman said that until she makes the demand, they can live there indefinitely. She feels honor-bound to let them stay since they come to church, however grudgingly."

As I shook my head, he turned to me and said, "Brad, for the Christian there's a fine line between thoughtful compassion and irresponsible emotion. Remember that."

Those were the memories of my week of odd situations, but I had a feeling that I'd see some more unpredictable events coming along soon enough.

I swung back up to South Dakota for a week of meetings in Hot Springs. This state was an adventure every time I drove across its borders. I believe I spoke in the Mount Rushmore State on three different occasions during my circuit riding time, and I always had a memorable experience. Those of you who have travelled across the Badlands and into the heart of this mysterious and wonderful state know what I mean.

The church numbered about fifty in attendance, and the week of meeting was an out-and-out effort to teach the people of the assembly how to reach others for the Kingdom. Pastor Mattish was a man who loved his people deeply and wished for them to grow in the Lord Jesus Christ. He greeted me as soon as I stepped out of the car, bounding down the steps of the church and actually chuckling in delight.

"Good to see you, son, *good* to see you!" He was in his late forties and of a stocky build, wearing a jacket with an open collar. He turned and swept his arms wide. "This is the mission field for me, Bradley. Hot Springs and anything nearby!"

Although my name isn't actually Bradley or Bradford, I found it a curious habit of people to call me 'Bradley' if they got excited. I'm not exactly sure why, but I can say with assurance that I got no pretense or dramatic overplay with Pastor Mattish. He was truly and sincerely committed to reaching the town for Christ.

I was given a double wide trailer for my week's lodgings. The trailer was located on five acres of land, and a long clay road led up to the property. The first two days' rain made the mile-long road slick and muddy, so much so that my wheel wells were clogged with earthy gunk for most of the week.

The pastor drove up to the trailer that evening, still bundling with energy. "Bradley, I want you to meet Neal, Bill, and Marilyn, my wife. Boy, I tell you, there'll be some exciting things going on this week. I just know it. God's going to move."

Marilyn moved about the trailer, preparing food from the refrigerator while Neal and Bill set the table and Pastor and I brought some ready-cooked meats from crock pots in the car.

"Now, I want you to pay special attention to Neal tonight," said the pastor. "He's been a Christian for only about, oh, two months or so, and he's really digging in, wanting to learn how to serve, how to pray, and how to read the Bible in a way to help him grow."

"Certainly," I replied. "How did you happen to meet him?"

"He came to church, stumbling in one Sunday morning," said the pastor, lugging a box of food. "He'd been a drug dealer over near Pierre for a number of years and was physically falling apart from a cocaine addiction. He was spiraling downward until at a bookstore he met a Christian girl named Carol who lived here in Hot Springs. He was intrigued by her character, how she stood up to him when he made advances to her, and how she let him know of her convictions. Carol was never impolite, he told me, but she never wavered either. Neal was intrigued by someone who had strength, because he said that nobody he knew had any kind of backbone or convictions. Carol did, though, and he was enamored. She really didn't have any romantic feelings for him, but she did befriend him. Stunned that anyone would ever consider him to be a friend with no strings attached, he dropped everything and moved down here. He dropped everything, that is, except his cocaine habit – he brought that to Hot Springs." We headed up the steps.

"But... well, I'll tell you more later." He opened the door so I could carry in my box. "Better yet, I'll let *him* tell you."

As we sat down to dinner, I looked at Neal. He was barely over five feet tall and well- dressed in a suit coat and tie, unusual for this rural community in the late summer. I could tell Neal had a hard life. His eyes were dreary, with dark bags underneath. His hands shook at times.

"Neal," I said as we ate, "Pastor tells me you've been a Christian for about two months."

"Yes, sir," he said, with a tone of respect, though he was about five or six years older than me. "I climbed out of bed one Sunday and decided that I was done with a life of indecision. I knew drugs were killing me, sir. I wanted some firm answers, and I wanted them before I finished out the day. There was a friend named Carol that I knew who had given me some direction on how to become a Christian, but she had moved away from Hot Springs, and I didn't feel that I should hang on one person to get me the answers I needed."

"I picked up a phone and started calling area churches and asking the person who answered the phone one simple question: 'how can I get to Heaven?'" Neal looked down at his plate and chuckled quietly. "Would you believe this, sir? Four successive phone calls - they hung up on me."

"What?" I was amazed. "Did they say that they were Bible-believing churches?"

"As far as what they put in the Yellow Pages," answered Neal. "And I began wondering: why does a church exist if it can't answer questions about Heaven?"

"Good question," said Bill.

"So I looked at the fifth ad in the Yellow Pages, and it was Pastor Mattish's church. I looked at the Sunday morning service time and knew I could make it, figuring I wouldn't let the man go until I got some answers. However, Pastor here gave a clear message and I made a decision that day."

"He was serious," said Marilyn, smiling.

"Yep," said Neal. "I chucked all the coke and the rest of the narcotics. Went clean and have been that way. Jesus made it possible, man."

"Amazing," I said.

"Amazing, but not unbelievable," said Neal. "Believe me, it happened."

As I nodded, Neal turned to the pastor. "Sir, I looked up the passage in Psalm 81, you know, the one that talks about singing to God because He's our strength. It also said something about God saying 'in your distress you called and I rescued you', and promises like that, but then it said that this was a, uh, a 'covenant renewal liturgy'." He smiled and pointed at Pastor Mattish. "I know you're trying to get me to learn something here. All right, tell me what it is."

The pastor pushed aside his plate and pulled a small Bible out of his suit coat. "Psalms 50 and 81 are both called covenant renewal liturgies, and they remind God's people about promises of protection that he gave them in the past. In turn, He wants them to renew their covenant of a great relationship – a time of worship that displays a dear friendship."

Bill nodded. "That's only fair. That's what we should be doing anyway. I mean, like getting serious with God."

"You've got the idea," said the pastor. "We get into church service and aim our worship to God through Jesus Christ. Psalm 81 reminds us that we don't just go through the motions, guys. We sing and pray and learn as a church for a reason, and that reason is to deepen our walk with God. It should never be routine."

Neal folded his hands in thought and looked up. "It's like having a birthday party just of the sake of the party, but it'd be stupid because nobody's birthday is recognized, right? Or like having a wedding only for the flowers and the music and the rice throwin' – it wouldn't make sense. That's like what's wrong with a serving that doesn't clearly point toward God. It should really be about honoring the God we worship. Each time."

"You got it," said the pastor.

"And that's what I want, each time I come to the building," said Neal.

The nights of the meeting went by and the people were responsive and active in the Word. They asked questions before and after the service. They met me at restaurants and drilled me as we chewed on A & W hamburgers and downed mugs of root beer. They stopped by the trailer, bringing deep discussions and plans of action to reach others. Neal was there among them in every available situation. He had taken his week of vacation from work so that he could get everything possible from this week of meetings. The people continued to seek and read. They wanted more than head knowledge; they wanted to feel God's power and be used by Him.

The week fairly flew by. On Thursday night as I concluded my message, I made a call to action.

"Tomorrow night is the final night of our meetings. I want you to try to bring someone to tomorrow night's meeting because I'm going to give a plain, clear John-chapter-three approach to salvation and how to get to heaven. How many of you will try to bring a friend, an acquaintance, or even a stranger?"

Virtually every hand went up in the room. Neal's hand was raised, and I could see on his face that this was a deeply serious commitment he was making.

Friday night was the final night of the meetings. The service started at 7 p.m. I was standing in the empty main auditorium at the top of the hour, totally puzzled at the lack of people, when Pastor Mattish burst through the door and yelled to me.

"You're wondering why nobody's come in yet, huh, Bradley? Well, I've been holding them all back in the parking lot. I want you to meet someone first!" With that, he slammed the door shut and then re-opened it grandly.

Neal came in alongside a tall, mop-haired man with a day's growth of beard on his face.

"Sir," Neal said to me, gripping his Bible and gesturing to the man, "I want you to meet Mike." Mike smiled warmly and even gave me a short bow.

Neal turned to look at him. "Mike accepted Jesus as his Savior five minutes ago." Neal turned to look at me. "I was able to lead him to Christ myself."

I shook hands with Mike, then took a step back and sat down on the front step of the stage. "Neal, you'd better tell me all about it." Mike was grinning ear to ear. Pastor Mattish and other people quietly slipped in the back of the auditorium, unknown to Neal, so that they could hear.

Neal stepped forward, cleared his throat and told us the story:

"Last night I was in the service, as you know, and heard you talking about reaching out to bring a lost person to the service so that they could hear about Christ. I raised my hand and made a promise to Jesus Himself that I would bring someone. I mean it – I promised that I would do so, since this was the last day you'd be here. And I prayed this to Jesus Himself so I wasn't taking this lightly."

"So this morning I got up and jumped in my pickup and went downtown into Hot Springs. They're having our annual Black Hills Festival and since there were thousands of people here, I pulled up into the big parking lot – it was a big field, actually – and made my way through the festival, inviting people. I figured I could get ten or twenty people to come. The morning went by and some people listened, other people ignored me, but nobody said they'd come. Well, I was a bit frustrated but not discouraged. I kept praying. Maybe seven or eight people would be fine, I thought. Noontime came and went, and I kept inviting people all through the festival, but still nobody wanted to come. Now I was at the point that I would settle on two or three to come to the service. Some people even openly mocked me, but still nobody agreed to come. Now I was praying hard, asking for just *one* person to come with me."

"The late afternoon was no better. Not a person, not a one. Well, I knew the service would start at seven o'clock and I knew I had to make it back here to the church on time. I was seriously hurtin' though. I had spent over eight, nine hours asking people and trying to get them to understand how important this was. Nothing."

"There was nobody in the field where the cars were parked, so I had just about given up. I wandered back to my pickup truck in the middle of those hundreds of cars and slumped in the seat, leaving the door open and praying a heartbroken prayer. I said, 'Lord, wouldn't You send somebody my way? You know I'm serious about reaching out to folks. Couldn't You send me someone in need?'"

"I reached out to grab my door and slam it shut when a man out of nowhere grabbed the door by the handle and asked me with an urgent voice: 'Mister, could you tell me how to get to Heaven?'"

"Well, I looked up, pretty stunned, sir. The man told me: 'I went through the hell of being in Viet Nam, seeing people die, and I haven't had peace in years. I've tried everything to get some peace, but I can't get it. I need peace in my life and in my soul, mister. I know I'm gonna die one day and I need to know. Mister, could you tell me how to get to Heaven?'"

He pointed to Mike, who was grinning ear to ear.

"I said to him," continued Neal, "brother, get yourself in the truck and I'll take you to a man who's going to talk about that very thing in five minutes. Well, he sure enough jumped in the cab but he said, 'I can't wait that long. I need to know now. I can't wait five minutes.' And so while we were driving over here, I was able to show him how to become a Christian and let Jesus take over."

Mike stood up and thumped his chest. "I'm a new man," he said. "I'm a new person."

"And you know, in another sense," said Neal, "I am too."

I knew what Neal meant.

95

As we sat on the carpet at the front of that small church with the people of the church piling in, crying and hugging, I had an astounding truth drive home into my heart and soul:

This is what I wanted to do for the rest of my life.

I wanted to do what Neal had just done. I wanted to reach out to other people.

I was tired of the social-centrism of Christianity where the "big-crowd excitement" was becoming the obsession of every church at the expense of actually teaching what God would have us to know. I had grown weary of the desire for congregations to make on-stage music the forefront of the meetings. I was tired of seeing pastors who wanted to gain prominence and power. I wanted none of that.

I wanted *this*.

No matter what my occupation or my situation in the future, I wanted to lead people to Jesus. I wanted Christ to guide me to people – any race, any culture, any financial status, any situation – and help them see the Cross. This was what I knew the Lord was showing me now. I wanted to be off the stage and onto the street-level eye-to-eye work of seeing people where they were and showing them how Jesus could lift them up.

I wanted to be like Neal, who cried in his truck and begged the Lord to show him someone who was hurting and searching – and God did.

6.

Michigan: Tea Kettles, Plans for a Band, and 32 Degrees Below Zero

The snow was already starting to fall as we boarded the bus in the Detroit parking lot. "You sit on this bus, Brad," called Dirk, his voice rising above the wind that was starting to whip up. "I'll be on the front seat of the other one." He checked his clipboard. "We have seventy–one teens in all. At each rest stop we'll double-check the numbers so we don't leave anyone behind."

Dirk was a tall, wiry college buddy of mine, now serving in his second year as the youth pastor of First Church of Elders Avenue, enjoying a fine ministry. He had carefully planned and spearheaded his very first winter retreat, and the teen response was enthusiastic. Dirk had also invited five other churches in the county and had asked me to be the main speaker at what they were calling their Polar Bear Breakout. All six churches would load their buses and meet up at a camp in the upper reaches of Michigan that evening for the opening service. It was now mid-afternoon as Dirk had finished packing his teens, adults and camping gear into two buses.

Dirk handed me an Army-green walkie-talkie. "If you need to contact me, use this," he said. These were the days before cell phones.

"Okay, Dirk," I answered, pocketing the walkie-talkie and pulling the parka tightly about me, trying my best not to shiver in the midst of these winter-seasoned folks. The truth was even though I was equipped with boots, scarves, gloves and thick layers, I was already cold ... and we hadn't even started yet. I looked across the street at the electronic bank sign. It showed a temperature of ten degrees Fahrenheit.

He gave me a thumbs-up and trotted towards his vehicle. Within a minute, both heavily-laden church buses were lumbering out onto the main drag that led to the Interstate. The driver turned on his wipers. I looked out the window and saw Dirk standing inside the front of his bus, balancing himself while the bus bumped and swayed, giving announcements and rules to his passengers as we swung up on the Interstate ramp.

Buses are part of some of my most vivid memories during my two-year journey around the country. More than once I was invited to speak at a camp location which dictated that I ride a bus along with the rest of the church group. These are prime times for me for two reasons.

First, some of the most in-depth conversations I've encountered came during an extensive bus ride. It might be the utter boredom of the trip that causes people to want to talk in rather deep conversations even though we're talking in a pitch just above the noise of the engines; remember, these aren't Greyhounds – these are school buses that have gone into retirement and were purchased by churches. No matter the noise – the group talks were fascinating. There have been times when teens or adults have piled into a tight circle so that we could have a "round table session" while on the way to a retreat location. There have also been many happy incidents where I counseled in a one-on-one session to someone in need. In many cases the bus rides have been even more fruitful than the camp experience itself.

Second, the bus will experience a breakdown. Pure and simple – the thing will drop a fan belt, cable, piston, windshield or roof. You church workers know what I mean; on any given trip the odds that a bus will experience a mechanical problem are high enough to make any Las Vegas bookie drool. If not a mechanical failure on the *outside* the bus, it is assured that something weird will happen *within* the vehicle.

Such was the case here. In fact, we enjoyed *both* delights on this Michigan trip.

The prospect of taking this winter camp expedition toward the upper part of Michigan was intriguing to me not only for the frostbite potential of the event itself, but also for a chance for me to watch Dirk. We had been side-by-side in a number of classes at college and I had seen his hair-trigger temper explode over very small things. He'd fume if his pencil broke. He'd grind his teeth if his quiz result was below average. He'd fly into a rage if his girlfriend was late in meeting him at the snack shop. Large things, small things would set Dirk off so easily that he'd developed a campus-wide reputation, earning the nickname Tea Kettle.

Here he was, in charge of a six-church event in numerous aspects: the travel, the lodging, the daily schedule and even the menu. I was going to make this a study in human behavior. Would Dirk handle the pressure?

I guess a bigger question, at the moment, was if I could get enough heat into my body. We'd been on the road for about twenty minutes and it seemed like they had the air conditioner on full blast. I was trying not to shiver, but the bus felt like an ice box.

"Excuse me," I leaned forward and spoke to the driver. "Could you crank up the heater a bit more? I think my toes are crystallizing."

"Ha ha," the jovial driver looked at me and laughed aloud. "Dirk said you were a funny guy. Cold feet, that's a good one." He shook his head. "No, friend, the heater's been broken on this bus for over a year. It's not that bad, really."

I grimaced. "Well, isn't there a way you can, like, open some sort of a vent and let the heat from the engine come in here and raise the temperature a bit?"

"Hee hee," he showed his showed his teeth and snickered. "Open a vent to the engine. You *are* funny."

I was trying to figure a gentle way to tell him that my intentions were not to entertain him, when we were interrupted by a passing pickup truck that was honking his horn and motioning for us to pull over. Since we were the lead bus, both vehicles found a safe place to stop on the shoulder and I piled out along with the other adults.

The fellow in the pickup walked back to us as he held his hands up. "Say, sorry to do this, but I thought you need to know, what with all those kids in the bus. You're pouring smoke out of your engine, and I can see your manifold is red-hot."

We peered into the engine to see the cherry-red glow of the manifold. The whole engine smelled of burning rubber.

"There's also something wrong with the belts," said our driver. "Look at how shredded they are."

"Here's some more smoke, right here, see?" Someone pointed to yet another problem as Dirk walked toward the bus engine.

The man shook his head and turned to us. "Look, I'm not much of a mechanic, but I know enough about cars and engines to see trouble. All I gotta say is that you don't want to be driving anywhere with all these kids and have problems like that."

I watched Dirk's face. This was Tea Kettle boy, remember. We all waited to hear his response.

He turned graciously to the mechanic guy. "Thank you, sir, for spotting this. You've really help us avert a disaster," he said, chuckling. The man nodded and walked back to his pickup truck. Dirk turned to our driver - the happy guy who thought I was telling jokes. "Pull into that truck stop right there," said Dirk, pointing to the place only a half a mile down the road. "I'll need to figure this out."

The truck stop was too small to handle an immediate influx of over seventy teens. Though the kids were well-behaved under the circumstances, they were everywhere chatting, laughing and buying up every Gummy Worm and package of beef jerky they could find. I saw Dirk over in the corner, working the pay phone.

"What can I do to help?" I asked. A few teens and adults were at my shoulder.

"I can't get a proper mechanic at this time of the evening," said Dirk, "and nobody's answering at the church. I can't get any of the staff on the phone, and we're cutting the deadline close to making it for this evening's meeting." He looked over my shoulder to a burly man in a Detroit Tigers baseball cap. "Jim, take the senior high school boys and start moving all of the luggage onto the second bus. Anne, take the girls and use this clipboard to get a head count and load the first bus kids onto the second one. Make room the best you can."

"*All* the teens on *one* bus?" asked Anne, taking the clipboard. She waved to four girls who immediately came to her side.

Dirk nodded. "Pack 'em the best you can and get on the road." He patted the second driver on the shoulder. "I'll stay here with the first bus until it's towed to a mechanic and I'll keep working the phones until we get another bus. Then we'll catch up with you and sort the kids out again."

The driver nodded and the adults went to work. Teens gathered and helped move the luggage and were soon wedged on the second bus, fitted as tightly as blocks in a Jenga game. I'm not sure if we were street-legal this way, but we were ready to move out.

Dirk winked to me. "When you get there, gather the teens in the main chapel and start if I'm not there by eight o-clock. You can handle it, can't you?"

"I'll get it rolling," I promised, and reached out to shake his hand. "An emergency like this, with a deadline to boot and you're as cool as a cucumber. No more Tea Kettle, huh? Dirk, what happened?"

He shrugged. "My anger was my ego acting up. That's the best way to tell you, Brad. I realized early in my ministry that if *I* kept getting in the way, I was shoving Jesus out of the picture. It was pure selfishness, and once I accepted the fact that it was not about me, I had a better grip on my anger issues." He waved me away. "Go, now. I'll catch up with you."

As I trotted out the door to the parking lot my breath was ripped away from the icy blast. "Oooof," I gasped to the driver. "The temperature's dropping, isn't it?"

"Yep," he said, pulling the door closed. "The waitress said they read the thermometer a few minutes ago and it was one below."

I realized we were on a different bus and a small hope rose within me. "Do we have a working heater on this bus?"

The driver chuckled. "No, it broke about two years ago."

"Look," I said desperately, "do you think anybody on the bus has a portable heating device? Like a battery-powered electric blanket?"

"Oh, you're the funny guy," said the grinning driver. "Dirk said you'd make with the jokes."

And so we headed out, packed like sardines. *Cold* sardines.

I was sitting in the front of the bus, now elbow-to-elbow and shoulder-to-shoulder with kids from floor to ceiling. Teens were jammed in the aisles and packed in fours on each seat. As the darkness settled in and we entered our third hour on the road, I noticed that the teens had settled into a routine of quiet talk and acceptance of the way things were. I had never seen such a large group of young people react so calmly to a strained situation like this. This was quite admirable to me – I began realizing that *the teens were imitating Dirk.* His newfound peace as a leader had made an impact on the kids, and they were giving the same reaction. I had often heard that after a time a youth group will take on the characteristics of its leader, and in some cases I had seen it played out: if the leader was edgy, the kids were edgy. If he or she was sarcastic, so were the group members. If the leader was an avid Bible reader, the kids took on that affection as well. But never had I seen such a dramatic emulation of a Christian character such as this. Dirk's change of heart was indeed changing lives of younger Believers.

I looked out the window, realizing that this trip might be one of the most peaceful church bus rides I'd ever enjoyed when word reached me from the back: a girl named Susie was sick.

Real sick, as in "vomity sick," I was told. And she needs to see if we can find a rest stop soon.

I stood up, and in the passing car lights I could make out who this Susan was. I remember her from the beginning of the trip, because Dirk had assigned her a leadership position due to her maturity even at fifteen years of age. As I had loaded my gear onto the bus I was able to chat with her and found her a joy to be around but also a bit on the delicate side. She didn't like to get her hands dirty or engage in the good-natured horseplay on the church lawn. I worked my way halfway back through the maze of kids and squinted. She looked pretty woozy.

I stumbled my way up front and chatted with the driver to see if we might be able to find a rest stop soon. As it would happen, the bus driver was due for a fill-up at a prescribed truck stop only two minutes away. I passed the word back that we'd be pulling over within a hundred or so seconds.

Word came back up to me that Susan might not make it. She was really queasy and might upchuck at any moment.

I looked and saw the neon sign for the truck stop over the hill. "If there's any way to keep her calm, do it," I told the kids next to me. We'll be off this bus in no time." I pointed dramatically. "Tell her we're going to be pulling over at that truck stop." I instructed the kids to exit quickly but safely through the front and back entrances once the driver had applied the brakes.

As soon as the driver swung in and come to a stop, I jumped off and gasped when the blast of cold wind hit me. The temperature sign said fifteen below zero. The teen group moved smoothly; the kids were leaping off the bus in rapid succession and heading into the building.

I looked up anxiously. Almost empty.

Two girls sprinted off the bus, followed by a sour-faced boy with a hoodie, and then there was Susie. She seemed calmer now, and was reflectively wiping her lower lip with the back of her sleeve. I realized that she was almost stupid with fatigue; she didn't seem to have a real grasp on what was going on.

"Susan," I asked slowly, "are you all right?"

The snowy wind seemed to wake her up somewhat. She blinked and looked at me. "I am now. It's okay."

"What's 'okay' with you? I mean, don't you need to, ah, throw up now?"

"Oh, no, I'm fine," she said in a very serene voice. "I already did."

"Oh, no," I groaned. I've had to deal with cleaning up vomit spills on buses before. "Where did you throw up? In the seat? On the floor?"

"No," she said, pointing to the sour-faced boy. "He had a hooded sweatshirt, so I just pulled the hood open and puked in there." She was so dizzy that she was completely unaware how gross this was.

"Hey," she suddenly exclaimed. "I feel all better!"

"How am I supposed to take this hoodie off without getting puke all over myself?" growled the sour-faced boy.

"Oh, Mikey, shut up," Susie said. "You're always complaining."

Somehow Mikey was able to extricate himself from the Hood of Vomit and escape a fate worse than death, and we were back on the road within ten minutes. The snow coming down harder, and the wind was rocking the overly-packed bus. The front windshield was slowly covering with an icy frost at the edges and the wipers didn't seem to keep up with the flakes sticking to the glass. I had great admiration for the driver of the bus as I saw him peering with squinted eyes into the darkness beyond the headlights; he seemed like a Michigan veteran was used to tackling this sort of visual nightmare. My nervousness was made worse when we left the relative lamp-lit safety of the Interstate and entered a state road, then a county road that had absolutely no lighting whatsoever.

The icy frost crept up and tightened his vision down to a central foot-wide spot in front of him. He hunched over and peered through the storm. I glanced at the other adults in front, who seemed to be taking this in stride. Was I being too edgy? I wasn't sure if I should say anything and appear to be a tenderfoot who jumped at every shadow, but I couldn't see how he was able to steer this bus with such limited vision.

I nudged the man next to me and tried to act casual. "That snow takes some, er, getting used to in driving, huh? Does it take you all some years to learn how to see through all of that winter mess?"

The man looked straight ahead and nodded. "Oh, you never really get used to it. In fact, I'm amazed at how he can see at all. I wouldn't be able to drive in weather like this."

I fairly leaped to the bus driver's side.

He was – I am not making this up – peering through a portal of around eight inches in diameter.

I cast aside any politeness now. I grabbed my scarf and started scraping away the frost on the inside of the windshield in front of him.

"Oh, thank you very much," he said without taking his eyes off of the road. "I was really having problems and I wasn't sure what to do. I could hardly see anything outside of the bus in front of us." He giggled. "It was a lot of guess work."

Despite there being no heat on the bus, I broke out into a heavy sweat. Collaring the nearest youth worker, I made them sit next to the driver and continually scrape the windshield clean to the far corners. I threatened them bodily harm should they cease from their labor.

We turned onto an even smaller road with ditches on both sides and farmhouses in the distance. "We're about an hour from the camp," called the driver.

I felt a tap on my shoulder. "Mister Brad? Can I talk with you?"

I turned to see a young girl with a ski cap and thick scarf standing in the aisle. She looked to be about seventeen or eighteen years of age. "I just had a few questions."

"Sure," I said, and made space for her to sit next to me. "What's your name?"

"Melinda."

"Good to see you, Melinda. How can I help you?"

"Well, I'm not sure how to go about doing something," she said. "You see, I want to go into a full-time ministry."

"Hey," I smiled. "Fantastic." It was always great to hear about a young person making such a commitment. "Serving the Lord is awesome, I can tell you from personal experience. So, tell me, Melinda, what type of ministry do you want to enter?"

"I want to start a band," she replied. "And I'll be the lead singer. I've thought this out, you know, and I want to gather some musicians together and travel around the country to youth groups and play and sing."

I sat back and nodded, wanting to put her to the test. "Okay. Why?"

"Because I have a good voice – well, really, people say I have a *great* voice, and it really captures people's hearts… that's what they also tell me." She shrugged. "And I already have two guys who said they'd join up with me. Brian plays the guitar pretty good, and Paul is a drummer." She looked at me. "So we're already getting things put together, you know?"

"Okay," I repeated. "Why?"

She paused and stared at me momentarily. "Well, I'm a poet, and I write nice lyrics. I've written a number of poems and I'm also good at putting together music… you know, a melody. I think groups around the United States would want to hear our ministry in songs, and we've talked about making a recording or two, and probably donating some of it to an orphanage. So… there, you see, I have the talent God gave me, and I want to get a band ministry going and travel."

I wasn't going to give up. "Why?"

She looked at me sharply. "Because God's given me a voice that's good, and I want to use this talent and go on stage. I won't let the success go to my head, I mean, I want to go full-time, but I can keep a pretty good attitude about this." She cocked her head to one side. "I don't get it. How come you keep asking me the same thing?"

"Because I want to know the *reason* behind this," I replied. "What is the outcome of this? How will Jesus be glorified? You keep telling me that this is a ministry, and *how* will it be a ministry?"

She wasn't getting it. "I have the talent of singing, and I want to organize a band and go sing at churches. We know some churches that will be willing to let us start a tour."

I turned towards her, trying to get her to understand. "Melinda, you keep telling me *how* you're going to get this band ministry going but you don't say *why*. To the Christian, a ministry points all efforts to Jesus Christ, to glorify *His* name. You seem to want to get a name for yourself. If that's the case, then this is kind of like a career, a job. For that matter, why even call it a ministry?"

She was losing her patience. "Listen, I could be up there with one of those big names. I've been told I have the talent, you know?" She turned and faced the front of the bus. "I want to be up there with them."

I wasn't sure I heard. "With *Him*? You mean, Jesus?"

"*No*." Her reply was curt. "With the big names in the business."

I looked toward the front as well. "So you want to get some fame?"

She nodded. "You want the truth? *Yes*."

I grinned. "Well, would you like to hear a story? It might help you out a bit."

She tilted her head a bit. "Well, all right."

"I'll tell you about my first brush with greatness," I said. "I was in the sixth grade at Hershey Middle School, I was the typical geeky kid with a big head, goofy teeth and a below-average athletic ability."

She snickered.

"Well, come to think of it," I continued, "maybe I *wasn't* typical. I don't remember many kids with heads as large as mine. I was a doofus of a kid, being ignored by the Inner Sanctum of cool kids. Especially the girls."

I held up my finger. "That is, until I won the all-school spelling bee." She smiled. "Yeah, my friend. That was grand. I remember it like it was yesterday. The school held the whole event in a community center theater and lined us kids up in rows at the front of the auditorium. One by one we went through the agonizing process of taking on words that suddenly became enemies. We had to take them on in the public field of battle. And, for once in my life, Melinda, I won. I can remember my last word for the win: *commercial*. Oooooooh, man. What a feeling. I finally won something. I remember standing next to the second place winner, a kid named Dave, and we were met by the principal of the school, a kindly bald man who always wore bow-ties. I won a Roget's Thesaurus, which took me about five years to understand what it was to be used for. Never mind that, though. I won."

"And here's what happened, Melinda..."

"... I entered into the realms of celebrity-hood. Kids waved to me in the hall. Teachers patted me on the back and smiled. My picture was in the newspaper. Even the lunch lady congratulated me and called me by name. And best of all, the Beautiful Kids asked me into their group."

"Must've been pretty cool," said Melinda.

"Well, yeah," I admitted. "But after a flighty day of head-rushing excitement, I soon came to the realization that I was not as smart as I was made to look. I couldn't even fool myself. In the spelling bee, I hit a good run of words that were within my capabilities, and I didn't freeze on stage. That was it. A week later in the State Spelling Bee first round, I realized how stupid I really was. I got crushed in the first round."

"I came to discover - as we all do sometime in our lives, many times more than once - that I was not the invulnerable, superior being I'd like to think I was. I just received a big batch of grace. I realized that it was not my prowess, but by the grace of God I won. There were numerous kids smarter than me. And I realized something else, as the flock of cooler kids came by to absorb me into their Winner's Circle." I paused.

"What's that?" Melinda asked.

I looked at her. "I didn't want to be with them. They strutted and posed and weren't ... well, *real*. I wanted to be among my own once again. Geeky, big-headed, buck toothed kids who talked with me and listened to me and goofed around."

She nodded.

"Then when we moved to Maryland and I entered middle school. I was still a dorky kid wearing hand-me-downs and high-water pants. I made a few friends who had the same kind of fashion sense as me, and we got along in our goofball ways."

"Well, they had a talent show, and I entered it doing a comedy monologue. Wouldn't you believe it, I won *that*. And suddenly, the Beautiful People wanted me to join up with them."

Melinda shrugged. "Did you?"

"No," I replied. "I had enough of the look-at-me crowd. I wanted honesty in my friendships and reality in my life. I didn't want to sit alongside any 'big names.' I looked at her. "And neither do you. It's not a real life. There's no peace. Peace is found in following God's ways, not your own desires."

Believe it or not, she smiled and nodded. "Thanks, Brad. You've given me something to think about." She rose and found her way through the mass of teens back to the rear of the bus.

"Here we are," called the driver, "all in one piece."

"Not funny," I said. He threw the door open and my lungs froze solid.

"Welcome!" shouted the camp director. "You're part of our camp's history as of right now!" He swung his arms wide. "It's *thirty-two below zero!*"

7.

North Carolina: Patience, No Preparation at All, and a Bone-Breaking Handshake

Jeremiah 29:12 - *"Then you will call upon me and come and pray to me, and I will listen to you."*

Like Neal, I had made a desperate, heart-wrenching call to God to serve Him and be a part of His work here on Earth. My call was after what felt like years of a fruitless, wheel-spinning going-through-the-motions period of my life.

It was terrifying. I thought I had lost God, and so I prayed. Prayed *hard*.

In my first ministry out of college I had attended a Christian leaders' conference in Mount Hermon, California where the theme of the evening's message was in reaching out to the lost people of California. Many of the Christian workers – myself included – felt a deep spiritual fatigue as we labored in the faith. Few places in America showed such a callous indifference to God as the West Coast. It was especially hard for me, being an Easterner – the culture as well as the spiritual make-up were two difficult mountains for me to climb. This conference was to be a time of refreshing and encouragement.

The speaker was a no-nonsense type of guy. Short and bespectacled with a machine-gun cadence to his speech, he adjusted his suit jacket and gestured toward us.

"You all feel worn out, don't you? Tired because of your sacrifice day to day, don't you? California's pretty much run roughshod over you."

We all nodded. *Yes, yes.*

He stepped to the side of the podium. "And you're weary of the way you're getting treated, how you get belittled, right?"

We nodded again. *Oh, yes, yes. We're so tired.*

He looked across the crowd. "Well, *get over it*. There are missionaries who are serving and sacrificing a lot more than you ever will, but *they're* not complaining."

Our heads snapped to attention.

He raised a finger and pointed it to the ceiling. "Let me ask you something. How many of you personally led someone to the saving knowledge of the Lord Jesus Christ this year? We're now in October, and I ask you: since January, how many of you have *personally* – not by preaching from a pulpit or on a stage – *personally eye-to-eye* guided someone to the Kingdom?"

The packed conference hall was absolutely still.

"Well, then," he said as he walked back to the lectern, "why don't you stop complaining and start praying about *that*?"

Man, that hit home to me. I was in my second year serving in Hollister and I was miserable over the fact that I had not been able to personally lead a single soul to the Savior. I had tried, but with all of the other duties of service I had let it become less and less of a priority. *But how could it change? I'm in a rut I can't get out of.*

I was broken. I stumbled out of the meeting room that night and wandered through the darkness across the conference center, shaken by what the speaker had said. But how could it change? What could I do?

I found an unlit chapel at one side of the campus and tried the door. Opening it, I quietly entered into the darkened sanctuary guided only by the moonlight coming in through the large stained glass window at the front. I fell to my knees. And I wept.

I cried so hard that I fell forward, face down on the wooden floor and called out to God. *You know I'm trying to serve. You know I want to lead people to your salvation. And You also know that here are so many chores and jobs and things that eat up my day hour by hour. What do you want me to do, Lord?*

I raised my head and, by the moonlight, saw the tears glistening on the floor.

Lord, you see these tears of honest anguish. I deeply want to do what You want in leading someone to Christ. I'm coming to you boldly and asking that You honor my request, Lord. Take it all over, Father. I've been trying so hard, and it's been a dead-end road. Take it over.

That was Saturday night.

On Monday morning I heard a knock on the door of my apartment. A girl of about twenty-one was collecting for the Red Cross.

"You're not from the area, are you?" she asked as I gave her a donation. "In fact, if I'm not mistaken, you're that new staff member at that church up the hill, aren't you? A youth pastor, am I right?"

"Yeah, you're right," I said. "Wow, word gets around fast in this town."

"Well, I kinda know about stuff that goes on in Hollister," she said. "My name's Sheila, and thanks for the donation." She turned to go. "I've been to every church in this town, really."

"Is that so?" I could feel the Lord's gentle push. "I mean, *all* of them, Sheila?"

"Yep," she said. "Jewish, Universalist Unitarian, Catholic, Mormon, Buddhist, B'hai faith…"

"Hey," I said. "Would you like to try one more? Special favor to me?"

She turned around again. "Where?"

"Up the road here," I said, pointing. "I'm speaking on Sunday and I'd like you to be my special guest."

"Well, uh, sure," she said.

And that Sunday she came. After I finished speaking and the service concluded, I came down to meet her. "Thanks for coming, Sheila."

"Sure, Brad. Hey… can I ask you something?

"Yes."

"Is Jesus the right way to Heaven? Seriously?" She turned her head and drilled me with her eyes. "I'm not kidding."

"He sure is, and I'm not kidding, either." I showed her the passage in John chapter 14. I let her read it herself.

She put the Bible down with finality. "Then," she said, "I want you to help me with this prayer."

And Sheila became a child of God, committed to His Kingdom, on that Sunday afternoon. God had given me an amazing answer to prayer. In fact, when Sheila came to my door and I was able to invite her, it had been the very next day we returned from the conference. More specifically, God had answered my prayer by giving me the answer within 24 hours... *right at my front door.*

And now I was going to see prayer work in stunning ways once again.

We were entering the final week before the school year would begin, and although it was still August, I could feel summer's grip letting loose. The air was a bit cooler as September approached, and I was enjoying my ride back into the Carolina territory. The trees hadn't started to change colors yet, but the anticipation of the high school football season and the fall decorations was already evident around the state as my car passed through the many little towns that make up North Carolina. I was feeling more relaxed and had been able to set my travel schedule so that it wasn't so manic. This was a good week as far as travel went, because I had just finished meetings in Chattanooga, Tennessee. I even had enough time to stop along the border and indulge in a rare treat for myself: boiled peanuts. I got one cup plain and one of Cajun-flavored boiled peanuts. A fine way to pass the time while traveling on Interstate 40, but trust me, you'll need to get to a car vacuum by the time you finish your second cup. Those wet shells really stick to everything, even the steering wheel.

My meetings in Chattanooga covered a number of different churches around the city's region, so I experienced the challenge of speaking and serving in a wide range of places of worship. My most challenging day was in the southern part of the city, when I entered the auditorium to speak on a Wednesday night to a grand total of five people in attendance in an auditorium that could hold well over five hundred. The evening after the service was spent in a heart-rending counseling session with the pastor, a man old enough to be my father, who was losing hope in his work. He had hit a wall as far as his church went, and his physical demeanor showed the wear and tear of his labors. He sought the Lord's leading and worked slavishly to help the congregation grow not only in numbers but also in spiritual progress. All of his hard efforts, however, were met with a big yawn.

My heart went out to him. This was not the first time I encountered a pastor near burn-out stage, but it didn't make it any easier. We ended in prayer and I left in my now-rickety Aspen, wondering about the position of pastor in American churches. In my travels so far, I had seen both extremes. I had met some of the laziest excuses for ministers, men who would fairly live on the golf course and spend hours lolling over long lunches at Chili's or TGIF Fridays. They wouldn't answer their phones, wouldn't prepare their messages responsibly, or wouldn't respond to the members' spiritual needs.

On the other hand, I'd seen men who would just about drive themselves into the grave with their sincere dedication to the work of the Lord. They saw the fields that were "white unto harvest," and worked almost around the lock in dedicated service to the Lord. My admiration for them knew no bounds.

What kind of pastor would be in this next church, I wondered as I made one more stop for gas at a country store that would make the front cover of any Cracker Barrel menu. I was getting the idea that this might be the most rural town I had visited yet; half of the country store's side walls comprised of rusty metal signs advertising RC Cola, Texaco gas and Chevy used parts. It was a quiet Sunday night, and I could see fireflies in the nearby fields. I had only thirty more miles to go along a road that had a barely discernable middle yellow line and no shoulders.

I drove through the miles of farms until I came to a weather-worn blue sign with white block letters welcoming me to the town of Cashlock. The population, it went on to say, was nine hundred and ten people, and the Lions Club met on the first Monday of every month. I looked beyond the sign to see first stand of trees completely hidden underneath acres of kudzu vine. I slowed down to meet the town speed limit of 20.

The sun had just set as I swung my car into the front parking lot of the red brick church on a Sunday evening. The church had cancelled Sunday night services so that I could meet with the workers and set the final details for the week's Vacation Bible School. It was to be the biggest event of the year, and the planning committee wanted no stone unturned. These people meant business.

I parked the car and stepped out with my notebooks as I returned the wave of a toothy thin man who bore an uncanny resemblance to billionaire Ted Turner. He was Pastor Rex Dennis and he grinned from ear to ear as I walked up the steps to the front porch. He slapped me on the back as we stepped inside the tiny lobby.

"Ah, we've been waiting for you, son," he said. "Great to have you here." He greeted me as if I were a long lost son returning home from war. Every third or fourth word he spoke was filled with a deep and sincere emotion. "I can't *tell* you how *good* it is that you're *here* with us this *week* for meetings and *especially* the Vacation *Bible* School program, *Brad*." One of the perks of this circuit riding ministry was that I made so many new friends of pastors in small churches. I soon found out that many of them did not have an acquaintance with whom they could just bust out laughing, talk freely about Biblical questions or simply share thoughts. Many pastors in rural churches lead lives with few or no good personal friends.

I instantly liked Rex Dennis. His friendly nature and kind demeanor won you over immediately. He made a polite gesture to his right and stepped back. "This is one of our church deacons, Alan Cartright." I reached over and shook hands with a fellow about my same age and realized Alan was making a point to squeeze my hand just short of the point of pain. "Hello," he said squarely, and although I do not doubt the sincerity of his smile, his eyes were boring into me for a reason I couldn't figure out. He was wearing a uniform of some sort. I withdrew my hand and felt it throbbing.

"Uh, are you in law enforcement, Alan?" I asked.

"No, he replied, "the state forestry service."

"Say, are you hungry?" asked the pastor.

"No, sir," I replied," I'm quite fine. Boiled peanuts did me in."

"Oh, okay," he said, "yes, of course." He was smiling as if I had just said the most ingenious thing ever. "Hey, come on in and meet some of our church workers."

"Are these folks part of the meeting this weekend about the Vacation Bible School setup?" The VBS was to be a big part of the last week of this summer. The pastor had written months before and said his volunteer staff of enthusiastic workers was undergoing extensive training and curriculum study even as he wrote the letter. He assured me that this group was one of the most Godly and sincere groups of people you'd ever want to meet.

"Yes, they are, and as I said, we're ready to go. We just kind of need you to take charge and pull it all together. Right this way," said the pastor.

"Down the stairs," said Alan.

I looked at my calendar and saw the details. "We're starting tomorrow morning... about nine-thirty?"

"*Exactly* at nine-thirty," said Alan.

"Yes," said Pastor Dennis, opening the door. "Nine-thirty it is. Oh, what a time we'll have!"

We both stepped through double doors into the wide basement, where everyone sat at tables and looked up at me in great anticipation, pens and pencils poised.

The pastor introduced me to the folks and turned to me. "I had told all of the people about the week's schedule. We'd have Vacation Bible School in the daytime and a Bible Conference-type of meeting every evening." He motioned for me to take the lectern as he sat down on the front row and picked up a pen and pad of paper.

"Well, sir, I've prepared the messages for this week's evening services," I said to the pastor as I pulled a pen out of my suit coat's pocket. "Since the evening's messages are all set, I'll concentrate on the VBS side of things. May I say that this is a privilege to be able to work alongside you all in a ministry as precious as one that aims for the hearts of children," I said. I opened my notebooks and lightheartedly rubbed my hands together. "Well, I need to catch up a bit. Due to my mobile nature, I was unable to receive your VBS curriculum and study it. Well, let's share notes first so we're all on the same page." I looked up. "Who will be teaching the main lessons?"

"Well," said Pastor Dennis, "that'd be you."

I looked at him for a moment. "Okay, then. Who will be handling the opening and closing ceremonies each day?"

Pastor smiled and looked benevolent. "We thought you'd also be able to do that."

I swallowed. "Well... I guess the best thing for me to do is to find out your theme, curriculum and artwork so that I can get a better handle on what each grade level is doing."

It got quiet. Too quiet. The people all smiled and looked at the back of Pastor Dennis' head. He cleared his throat.

"Brad, we spent some time looking at all of the Vacation Bible School material that the many publishing companies offered and, well..." He put his pen down and clasped his hands together. "...we felt that they were overly compartmentalized and even rigid. The more we studied the samples that were sent to us, the more we were convinced that there was an abundance of artwork, lessons, skits, and crafts, but no real room for the spiritual freedom we want to have." He tilted his head. "The publications were just too confining."

I shifted on my feet and looked around the room. "So, if I understand you, then you're telling me..."

"Yes," said Pastor Dennis. "We just threw out the idea of purchasing any curriculum and thought we'd follow however the Lord would want you to go."

I blinked and shifted on my feet again. "You're saying that you have absolutely no curriculum or artwork – "

"That's correct."

"No crafts or Bible lessons?"

Pastor Dennis nodded, smiling that nice smile.

"Not even an idea for refreshments?"

The rest of the pleasant people room smiled at me while shaking their heads "no."

I coughed lightly, trying to remain calm. "And this is a town-wide event that will be starting tomorrow morning, right?"

The pastor looked at me and winked. "That's absolutely right, son. We're here to follow your lead. Lead us on, then, good sir!" He picked up his pen again. "Now, where do you want us to begin?"

I gazed across the rows of genial faces looking to me for guidance and tried not to laugh uproariously. They were totally unprepared, and they wanted me to gather everything together, depend on God for the construction, and create a week's worth of meetings in ninety minutes... with the first day of meetings happening the next morning.

I wiped my face with my hand. I'd tried to walk into a situation without any preparation before and it just didn't work. Not at any time in my life.

For instance, as I entered the second grade, my dad was band director for the local high school and was pushing for me to find an instrument to play. For some reason I cannot fathom - it may be because it was the only other instrument sitting around the house - I chose the baritone.

The *baritone*. That piece of metal was bigger than me.

After the first week of band practice I hated it. I got bored of daily practice. The thing gunked up too much. But worse, the baritone is the school bus rider's nightmare. Shoving and pulling that thing onto the bus was an embarrassing and frustrating tribulation to an uncoordinated elementary school kid who's still trying to understand how to walk without falling down. I detested taking that thing to school. Why couldn't I have chosen a trumpet? Or a harmonica? A kazoo? I'm amazed I didn't need professional counseling.

Well, I hung on with that thing through the third grade, sliding into fourth chair (out of four) and not caring that I was probably shaming my dad into exile.

But here's the weirdest thing: when our homeroom teacher asked for talent entries for our little classroom Christmas party, I volunteered. Again, my actions were inexplicable. I don't know what I was thinking.

I couldn't even read music, let alone get a good note out. Nevertheless, I thought I could wing a rendition of Silent Night – through a special advantage. I am not making this up. I had the answer: *I would pray.*

I thought God would give me the talent. That's the truth. I practiced not a lick, but the night before the party, I forced my brother Brent to pray with me that God would give me the ability to pull off a stunning performance and be proclaimed God's virtuoso at Dallastown Elementary School.

Well, of course it didn't happen. Silent Night takes like, how long, two minutes to play? That is, if you know what you are doing.

It took me longer than ten.

Don't get me wrong - the class loved it. Wouldn't you love it if you were watching your fellow third grader go down in flames? I rolled my eyes trying to figure out what the next note would be, blowing notes at random. I coughed into the mouthpiece, emitting a sound like a hippo with severe gastric indigestion. I sweated and fidgeted, because I was *sure* I could wing this thing, because *God could do anything*, right? Wouldn't you, a low-self-esteem-suffering kid with huge ears and clod feet, love to see one of your classmates fall apart in front of you? I was a hero and a goat at the same time.

Prayer became clearer to me after that. I learned - and this is the truth - that God is not the end product of a magician's trick. He's not to be pulled out of a hat for self-fulfillment. He wants to *talk with us*, not be yelled at or commanded about. Yet some people still feel like I did in that baritone recital - God is a switch to be turned on and off.

Now that's what I saw was going to happen here in Cashlock, North Carolina. Would we all be taunting God into coming up with a plan that we didn't responsibly prepare?

No. We couldn't let this program fall apart. These people were not irresponsible, nor were they stupid. They meant to work every bit as hard with the deadline looming.

I would do the best I could while we got a boiler room of prayer warriors to get things rolling. I took a quick count. There were twenty people in the room.

"Okay, then, pastor," I said as authoritatively as I could. "I need you to select four people who will go into a side room and start praying for the success of the ministry to children this week. After fifteen minutes we'll rotate until everyone has been on their knees and called to the Lord for His leading." As the pastor turned and selected people, I went over to the white board behind me and started writing furiously.

"Our curriculum will be right out of the Bible, and we'll all stay together in the same room for our teaching – no breaking into smaller groups. I will teach on John chapter one on Monday, John chapter three on Tuesday, John chapter twenty on Wednesday – "

"Oh, right," said Alan, "the whole week will be the life of Christ from the book of John."

"Yes and no," I said. "Yes, the life of Christ, but not all from the book of John. Thursday I'll speak from the book of Revelation in the first and nineteenth chapter – we'll see Jesus as the warrior and the victor over all – and then on Friday we'll wrap it up by looking at John chapter fourteen and Revelation chapter twenty-one: the new home provided for us by Jesus, called Heaven."

I looked around. "We'll need crafts to make some artwork about Heaven."

A young lady with braids raised her hands. "Er, my name's Sarah. In another church I used to do crafts and I can get the kids to make pictures of heaven with cotton and construction paper. Then we'll work on some finger painting the next day. I have tons of supplies."

"Great, Sarah," I said. "We need to make a treasure chest for prizes as well. And lots of hard candy." A burly man in the back waved his hand. "Mike's my name. Consider it done. I have a brother in the candy business over in Raleigh. He uses my warehouse to store some of his goods. I have an old Army trunk, too."

I was getting excited. Things were coming together, and most importantly, the folks were pulling it together with their own ideas. As inconceivable as it may seem, within ninety minutes we not only filled our individual notebooks with the week's minute-by-minute plans, we also had stacks of food and crafts being hauled in as Mike worked the phones from the corner of the room, calling on church people to bring in donations. The whiteboard was filled with the special games we would play and other ideas that would fill out the week. Alan would be in charge of outdoor games, Sarah would head up the crafts, Mike would oversee the refreshments for the kids... the whole VBS project was looking good. I fell into bed that night completely worn but with the alarm clock set for an early rising time. The whole town knew that today was the day.

Or did they?

On Monday, by nine-thirty all of the workers were in place and ready for the ministry to kids. Except that there were no kids.

None.

At nine forty-five I walked over to Pastor Dennis, who was wearing a batting helmet with Marvin the Martian antennae bouncing around on it. "Pastor," I said slowly, "What kind of advertising did you do to announce the VBS week?"

"Well," he said, "we didn't feel that we should go about it with the usual man-made ways like the newspaper and fliers. We felt the Lord would bring the kids in." And he gave me that smile again.

I took off my sailors cap and rubbed my face for a full minute. "I'm going to need everyone to leave except for Sarah and Mike. They stay here with me."

"What are we supposed to do?" demanded Alan. He was wearing a giant foam pumpkin on his head.

"I want you to get in your cars and go see parents and start bringing kids in. We will kick back the unofficial time to ten-thirty." I looked at the rows of people. "Now go get in your cars and find the kids. This is like the Biblical command. Go into the highways and hedges and *bring 'em in!*" My volume was divided between an energetic exhortation and sheer frustration, but I don't think this group of eager country folks could pick up on the latter. After they piled into their cars – so help me, some of them were actually whooping, too – I knelt with Mike and Sarah and prayed. First we prayed for a good return and second we prayed for God to be honored and the glory brought to Him (while I silently prayed that I wouldn't burst out in a primal scream).

I knew God was teaching me patience, even when I felt justified for being impatient.

By ten thirty, the cars came back and twelve kids spilled out and came in running. A second car came in ten minutes later with six more children. Another child wandered in with his parents after hearing the commotion on the streets and so we finished Day One with twenty-three little ones. I must admit, I was amazed.

On Day Two at exactly nine-thirty there were forty children attending, singing, and memorizing John 14:6.

On Day Three we counted up forty-six young ones.

On Day Four we were amazed to register sixty-five kids. This was as large as the church's whole membership.

On the final day, I was amazed as the little church auditorium was packed with eighty-seven children.

Even more exciting was the fact that dozens of little ones had made decisions for Christ and whole families were committed to attending the church once they saw the care and devotion the members had for the kids.

The stories, the teaching, the games, even the food all came together under God's blessing. It was indeed a good time of ministry.

The week was over and Pastor Dennis was smiling as broad as ever. The evening services were just as exciting, but that's a story for another time.

"Brad, the church has passed the hat and wants to give you a love offering for all you've done." As I thanked him and got into the car, he leaned against the roof of the Aspen and peered in. "Oh, I almost forgot to tell you. You'll be going right by the state park on your way out. Alan would like for you to stop by for a minute."

I pulled into the parking spot in front of a small brown-and-tan building with a prominent RANGER'S STATION sign in front. The door was open and Alan was sitting behind a desk, painting on an easel.

"Come on in," he said as he dipped his brush onto the palette. "Oil painting is my hobby, and I like to try my hand at it a bit every day, whenever I get a coffee break," he added in a voice, to my surprise, that didn't have the monotone or bite that I was used to hearing from him.

"Hey, thank you for the work you did this week," I said as I took a seat. "I know you took vacation days to serve, and that's a special sacrifice that didn't go unnoticed."

He put down his paintbrush and shook his head as if to wave off the thanks. "I asked you to stop by because I needed to say something." Alan folded his hands and I could tell he was searching for the right words. He looked out the window and gathered his thoughts before speaking carefully and deliberately.

"I was raised in a military home," he said finally. "My father was very strict but not wholly without compassion. He was an Army man all the way, rising through the ranks because he knew how to give orders and how to take them."

"One thing I learned from the time I was an infant was to adhere to a plan once you made it. You drew out the strategy and you never veered from it. *Never*," he added with emphasis. "To change course was to invite disaster. It showed weakness."

I could see where he was going with this. "Alan, when I came in on Sunday night –"

He waved a hand. "And then on this Sunday night you come marching in here and grab this whole program by the tail and start throwing ideas up on the board, changing this, changing that, adjusting here, doing things on the fly... going against everything I've ever been taught. It pure and simple drove me crazy. I was angry, I was frustrated, and I was confused."

I clenched my teeth.

He sat back. "And I saw how wrong I was."

My eyebrows raised.

"I came to realize that throughout my life things don't go according to plan, and the surest way to failure is to keep plowing ahead on the path that desperately needs adjusting. I saw it this week with the way the pastor put you on the spot. I also saw it when the little boy Ryan couldn't grasp the plan of salvation through the eyes of Nicodemus in John chapter three, so Sarah adjusted it and showed him Jesus' promises about a home in heaven. Adjustments like that. Like when Mike ran out of hot dogs and had to make the rest of the sandwiches out of peanut butter and jelly."

Alan was silent for a moment and then looked up at me. "I needed you to know that your ministry this week was mainly with me. I was grieving for years because I thought this was the way I was supposed to live - unbending - and yet I knew it wasn't practical. I needed to see a real-life example before my eyes."

He reached out his hand. "Thank you, Brad. This week was a great lesson for me."

And this time he didn't try to mangle my hand.

8.

California: Peeling Potatoes and a Big Forgiveness Story

As I crossed the California state line and pulled into the welcome center, I could feel the cool breezes wafting across the open field near the highway. Autumn was on its way, and with its coming, many churches arranged their social calendar to greet the new season. A number of congregations were setting up special events like Homecoming Festivals or Fall Banquets. Youth groups were holding Back to School parties and special days. I received many invitations to speak at these occasions if I should happen to be in the neighborhood.

Under other circumstances, I would jump at the invitation. Not right now, though. I was heading to Oakland to stay at a rescue mission for two weeks.

Not due to financial problems, mind you, or for the lack of a place to sleep. In the last months while picking up highway hitchhikers and helping the homeless the best I could, I had developed a burning in my soul to go the extra mile. I wanted to reach out into the world of the downtrodden and destitute. True, I'd been spending most of my travels in assemblies of folks who were below the line of middle-class income, but I needed to experience the lowest level possible. I wanted to see God's work being done among the drug-dependent and the hurting. I wanted to be among them.

I had asked for some opportunities to speak to the Red Street Rescue Mission residents, and with that request I also asked I might become one of them during my stay. For the half-year I'd been on the road, I'd been able to roll up my sleeves and do more than speak, and in truth it was refreshing to be able to help an assembly and its pastor with various services like hospital calls and visits to shut-ins. But I also found out that I had just as much joy in the other odd jobs around the church, like cleaning out attics, mopping floors, setting up tables for a banquet, helping work on a church bus engine or running games for a children's program. I was trying to avoid the speaker's prima-donna stereotype that had pervaded the Christian community. I was very uneasy of being put on a pedestal – after all, why was I better than anyone else? I found it quite uncomfortable when I would travel to a town's church for a week of meetings and be expected to do nothing more than sit, chat, and eat until the hour I preached. On more than one occasion I was treated as if I were a celebrity about to take a stage for a theatrical production, and I had to gently inform the folks that I couldn't possibly handle that role. The people didn't mean anything wrong by it; it's just the way they had assumed a visiting speaker should be treated.

I learned to be repulsed by that stereotype, and I still feel that way today. I was seeing the workaday world in all of its headache-inducing reality, and I was humbled. I saw people who were doing back-breaking labor in construction sites, sweating out unforgiving deadlines in the corporate world, taking care of a household of children, slaving in overtime hours and facing the world's daily grind. People would work a full week's labor and then have enough energy to teach a Bible class, run the nursery, or drive a bus for the church. I had no reason to think that my day should be any easier than theirs. No, I wasn't going to be escorted around. Besides, it did very little good to sit - that wouldn't be the way to see God in His many avenues of blessing and mysteries. I wanted to mingle and work and sweat and tire and talk. And listen. Listen a lot.

It puzzled many friends of mine, but the fact is that's why you'd find me in a barn shoveling horse manure with Georgia farmhands out or in a field avoiding a bull while chopping firewood with a Tennessee family. I helped clean churches in Pennsylvania, sweep floors in Minnesota and set up summer camps in Maryland. It was all fun because it took off the puzzling veneer that had been added to travelling Christian speakers.

Please don't feel that I'm trying to enhance my reputation. I'm truly expressing my opinion about what a traveling minister can do for a small church. And as far as enhancing my reputation – well, with looks and abilities like mine, brother, there's no hope. So let's move on.

I requested a two week stay at the Red Street Rescue Mission in Oakland, California. I struck an immediate friendship with the director, Ed, who had been serving here for almost a decade. Ed was a slight, small man with a receding hairline, a generous beard and a voice that so gentle that it made me wonder how he could rule with authority in a place like this.

His office was a book-lined room located in the very center of the rescue mission, strategically placed so that he could be available to any area of activity. Ed shook my hand and motioned for me to sit in the metal chair across from his desk. "All right, Mr. Zockoll, let's see what we can do. We have a guest room for visiting speakers and other guests of the like. You can stay for up to two weeks," said Ed.

"Thanks, I *would* like to stay two weeks, sir," I said, "but I want to stay in the dorms with the rest of the guys."

Ed looked up. "Our speakers never do that. Why do you?"

I didn't want to appear high-minded, but I was fervent in my request. "Well, if I'm going to speak with them, I want to know more about where each man is coming from. I don't want to be an in-and-out speaker. After the messages, I want to walk over and have a discussion, be available. It's important for me to see what their day is like, what problems they face, and to talk with them one-on-one while I sit alongside them."

Ed was about to speak, but he stopped and leveled a stern gaze over my head. I turned around to see a large grizzled man standing in the doorway. "Gimme something to eat," the man mumbled.

"No, sir, I cannot do that. It's past the chapel and meal time," said Ed. "You've been here numerous times. You are fully aware of when we have the chapel and meal times."

The man glared. "Come on, I'm hungry."

Ed's voice took on a no-nonsense timbre and volume that surprised me. Gone was the gentle lilt to his voice. He was all business now. "*No*, sir, you are *aware* of the rules. The line-up time was at eight o'clock. You'll have to wait until noontime for the lunch meal. You've been here before. You *know* the times. They're even posted outside."

The man growled. "Then gimme some money so I can eat."

"*No*, sir!" Ed snapped. "I will *not* be a part of your drinking problem. You have a wife and children at home, and I know fully well you'll take that money and spend it on drink when your family needs to be fed. You'll not receive any money. *No*, sir."

"Why, you – "The man stepped in the room and raised an arm, heading toward Ed.

Ed never flinched. He looked the man in the eye and called out. "Jack!"

From out in the hall came the biggest Arnold Shwarzenneger-like arm I'd ever seen, extending through the doorway at a snap and grabbing the grizzled man by the collar. In one quick motion the arm belonging to "Jack" jerked the man off of his feet and pulled him backwards through the doorway.

It was over in a second. I shook my head, but Ed acted like nothing had happened. I found out later on that he had been cruelly beaten in the hallway years before by some intoxicated thugs. Because of that incident, the staff had made 24/7 bodyguard protection for him. I was to find out soon enough that the men loved and watched over Ed. They knew he had dedicated his life to helping them see how Jesus could lift them out of the daily hell in which they struggled. They thought the world of him.

Ed nodded thoughtfully. "Okay, I can see what you want to do. You want to be a Guest." "Guest" was the name of the men who signed in for help from the mission. They were not Staff, they were Guests.

I bobbed my head. "Exactly, sir."

"Don't call me 'sir', Brad, call me Ed. Okay then," said Ed, scribbling something on a piece of paper. "Park your car out back in the wire fence safety area and bring in your duffel bag. I have a bunk bed for you, where you'll be in a nice cozy room. With seventy other guys."

I parked my car and walked into the bunk area, where I was given a place in the corner of a large hall with over thirty-five bunk beds. Next to my bed I was given space in a small bedside nightstand with two drawers. The bottom drawer was where all my belongings were to be stored. No locks. I had the bottom bunk below a young black fellow with dreadlocks and a melodic laugh named Herbie, who had become a Believer and was now in his second month of being free from heroin. Next to me was

Russ, a stocky fifty-year old Native American with short-cropped hair, amazing strength and a palpable fear that he would fall back into alcoholism. His morning devotional times would have a deep impact on me. Many a time I would turn over in the early morning hour to see Russ kneeling beside his bed and lifting his hands in deep devotion to God, silently moving his lips and crying quietly.

Above him was Carl, a lanky twenty-seven year old African-American who had become a Christian two weeks ago. Carl had been through the worst drug dens in the city and had narrowly escaped death more than once. He was fervent about how to learn more about the Bible, but had a serious difficulty with his reading skills.

Herbie came in and smiled widely. "Brad, right? The Man tol' me what you were gonna be doing here," he said. "That's cool. I got a lot of Bible questions to ask you."

I tucked my shaving kit in the drawer. "Well, I hope I can answer them for you. Any way I can, I want to be a help, Herbie."

"I'll show you aroun' later on," said Herbie, "but first you gotta get something to eat, man. I'm with kitchen crew, and we serve the guys who come in." He led me down the hall and explained. "See, the men come in three times a day at a certain time, and if they're late, they don't eat. Nobody just wanders in here and eats whenever they want – that don't teach anybody discipline, see? They come in and hear a chapel message first, before they come in to the big dining hall to eat." He opened the door and led me into a smaller checker-tiled room with two long tables, almost filled with workers. "The chapel times are eight in the morning, twelve noon, and five at night. While they hear the message, we get the food out on the serving line so it's hot and ready to go."

"You're not staff, though?" I asked.

"No, not staff," Herbie said, pulling out a chair. "We're kitchen help, and so we're just called 'workers', but it's a position that gives us extra time. You see, you can only stay for two weeks in a row. Then you gotta leave for a week before coming back – that keeps guys from making this a home and not tryin' to get a job or do something with their lives. Us workers, if we serve in the kitchen, we get to stay for three weeks in a row."

Herbie turned to the workers. "Hey, everybody, this here's Brad. He's a Bible teacher guy and he'll be working with us and teaching in the afternoons. Or something like that."

The workers smiled and nodded. "Hey, nice tan," said an older man who was toying with a cigarette. He winked as the other men chuckled. I looked around to realize that I was the only Caucasian in the room. "Thanks," I replied.

Herbie was introducing me around the table, with fellows nodding and taking long puffs on their cigarettes. I learned that with many of the recovering alcoholics, smoking was one of the ways they found a replacement for the bottle. Virtually every man on staff – except Ed – was a smoker.

"This is Steven."

I nodded. "Hey, Steve."

Steven tipped his cigarette and smile. "Brad-man. Okay, then."

"This is Ben."

"Hi, Ben."

"Hey, man."

Herbie nodded toward a muscular man of about thirty years of age, right across from me. "This here's Ronald."

"Hey, Ron," I said.

He glared at me and didn't answer right away. When he did, it was through clenched teeth. "My name's not Ron –it's *Ronald*. You understand?"

"Okay, I got it ... Ronald."

He still glared and repeated as if I hadn't heard him. "My name is not *Ron*. Never has been, and never will be. It's *Ronald*. Got that?"

The older man named Ben looked at the wall and talked slowly. "Slow it down, Ronald, slow it down."

Ronald's head snapped to one side. "Why *should* I? People don't know what's it's like not to get respect. They don't know what it's like to have money and still be turned away from a hotel in Los Angeles near midnight. No reason for it except for my color. No reason. No respect. Some people don't understand that."

Another man looked at his plate and pushed a piece of meat with his fork. "Let it go, Ronald."

"I ain't gotta let it go."

I kept my gaze on him. "I'm sorry, man. Ronald's the name. I'll remember that."

He stood up and grabbed his plate. "See that you do." He stormed out.

The room was quiet while men puffed on their cigarettes. Ben sighed. "He's a Believer but lots of baggage. He's gotta realize Jesus'll take care of that."

"Mmm-hmmm," agreed someone in the back corner.

Steve shrugged and looked at me. "He's carryin' a lot of hurt." He looked down. "To people like you."

Herbie shook his head. "Ronald's been here almost ten days now, been a Christian longer than that, but some racism down in L.A. is stickin' in his memory and he can't let it go. He looks for a target. You're the nearest thing, I guess."

I didn't respond. I felt it was best not to. I just nodded.

Carl piped up. "Hey, are you gonna talk about the book of Revelation?"

"If you want me to," I said with a grin.

Ben bobbed his head. "I have a lot of questions about that book, I do."

"When are you gonna start?" asked Carl.

I pulled my New Testament from my back pocket. "When do you want me to start? Now?"

Carl cackled. "Now."

"Then now it is." I flipped open the pages.

And in the back kitchen area of Oakland's Red Street Rescue Mission, I taught my first lesson about the wonders of Heaven as found in Revelation chapter twenty-one, answering as many questions as I could through the clouds of smoke. At one point

I could see Ronald drift by and peek in the door. I made no attempt to let him know I saw him.

The study went on for two hours. We took a break, stretched and as soon as the fellows sat down they demanded to be taught the book of Daniel. The Daniel study went on for another hour.

Later on in the day, Carl and I were washing dishes and he scowled, thinking hard. "Hey, preacher, talk to me about this: I get puzzled on how I can be a Christian and not go crazy."

"What do you mean?" I asked.

"Well," he said as he stacked some plates, "our mind is supposed to be on Jesus all the time, right? A preacher told us that we should have our mind on Christ always. Then how can I talk if I'm constantly repeating the name 'Jesus' in my mind. How can I talk to someone if I keep repeating Jesus, Jesus, *Jesus*?" He picked up another dish and shook his head. "About to drive me mad."

"Ed," I said, "the life we live is centered on Jesus, but you don't need to keep constantly, physically repeating His name around the clock in order to be aware of Him. Look, it's like you're an American, right?"

"Right."

"And you're not Chinese, Italian, Canadian or Russian, right? Your lifestyle, language and outlook are completely American?"

"Right."

"Well, you live in that freedom and in that way of life, and you get to enjoy it, too. But that doesn't mean you have to keep repeating 'I'm an American, I'm an American.' That's *in* you. It's the same way with Christ. Your freedom, your outlook and your decisions in life are totally based on Jesus. That's what it means to have your mind on Christ."

Carl's shoulders sagged in relief. "Man, that's good to know. I wasn't sure I was doing this right." He turned around and threw a towel to Herbie, who had just walked in. "Here, you, make yourself useful."

Herbie scowled but picked up a bowl. "Don't get y'self uppity. I've been a Christian longer than you, old son."

"What's that supposed to mean?"

Herbie grinned. "I don't know. I was tryin' to think of a comeback."

I laughed and rinsed a stack of pots. "Carl, are you from Oakland?"

"Yep," he said, "born and raised here, dropped out of high school even though I was told I had a pretty good talent in art. I started into coke when I first got an apartment in West Oakland - if you could call it an apartment. More like a filthy room with a bath that never worked. It's bad stuff over there on the western side of town, brother."

"*Real* bad stuff," said Herbie.

"You're tellin' me," said Carl. "But I eased off the drugs an' I tried to get my life together, y'know? An' life was okay, because I like people. An' I like to smile."

"Yeah, he's always smilin'" said Herbie. "Nobody stays mad at Carl."

"Is that so?" I asked.

"True," said Carl. "Whenever I'd go to the bus stop, I'd usually get into a conversation with someone, usually a lady, and start laughing. Like I said, I was easing off drugs, but I'd do a little something here or there."

"Tell him about the guy with glasses," said Herbie.

"I was getting to that," said Carl, turning off the water. "Anyway, I was on the bus heading home to my apartment and on the same line was this guy who lived above me, a guy with glasses. Never did know his name, but for some reason he got to not liking me."

"Why?"

"Don't know for sure, but it may be that he thought I was getting drugs where he couldn't, or that maybe I was talking too much with a lady-friend of his." Carl wiped his hands on a towel. "One day on the way back on this bus, he starts raggin' on me, trying to get me mad. But I wouldn't, I kept smiling, 'cause it was a good day. We got off the bus and I was talking with a lady and this guy kept yelling, but I kept smiling so he went upstairs to his place. Well, it was cooler outside than in my place, so I sat on the front step of the stairway, talking with some folk. An' you know what that guy did?"

I shrugged.

"He brings down a knife and starts slicing on me," said Carl, shaking his head. "Slices me up one side and down the other. I'm not fighting him, but I roll over and I'm holding onto myself because I'm bleeding so bad."

"Show him, man," urged Herbie.

Carl pulled off his shirt and I gasped aloud. His torso was covered with thick, snake-like scars. One ran from his navel up over his shoulder. One was a fierce slash down the middle of his back. Another ran from his armpit over to his lower rib. Still another traveled from his collarbone down to his hip. I counted over eight thick pinkish scars.

"I was dying on those steps, and he folds up his knife and goes upstairs like nothin' happened." Carl blinked. "I lay there and called for help, bleeding all over that sidewalk, trying to hold my sides together, 'cause it felt like I was fallin' apart. An' nobody would help me, even make a call." He looked away.

"Carl, what happened?" I asked.

"Believe it or not," he poked the sink with his finger, "the only one to help me was the bus driver. I lay there until the next bus pulled up and the bus driver looks out and calls the ambulance. Man, it was close. I was feeling myself slip away. Light-headed, like they say."

He looked over at me. "Took weeks and weeks at the hospital, but you know? The chaplain, he helped me out. He told me how close I came, and I started asking questions, you know, about Heaven and Jesus and the Bible. I got answers." Carl smiled. "In a way, that knifing was a good thing for me. Can you believe I just said that?"

I hauled bricks and scrubbed floors with the guys. I heard about alcohol and cocaine, heroin and meth. There were stories about shattered families, extreme poverty and tragic childhoods.

One of the most puzzling people I met was Greg, a large blond-haired fellow who wore a three-piece suit and parked his shiny Porsche in the gated secure area every morning. Greg would greet me with a loud hello and be on the front row whenever I'd speak, Bible in hand. He didn't stay in the bunk beds, but he did come in for the day, every day during the two weeks of my stay. It seemed odd to watch him in his attire, eating and chatting with men who wore ragged shirts and ill-fitting pants. I asked Ed about him.

"Greg's a top salesman, lives across the bay, but a combination of alcohol and various recreational drugs nearly cost him his family and his job. Somehow he ran afoul of the law as well. He went before the courts and volunteered to come over here. He's been serious about it, and we've been seeing progress little by little." Ed turned to me. "You don't have to be poor to have these problems, Brad-man."

Ronald walked by, brushing my shoulder with his arm, glaring at me. It was as if he were saying *I don't forget. And I won't forgive.*

The next morning, we were sitting out back, peeling potatoes and listening to Carl try to get Russ to talk about his high school wrestling days. I wiped my hands on my ragged T-shirt, realizing how pleasant it was to go without a suit coat for a few weeks. Russ was grunting and starting to peel carrots when Herbie came through the door. "Hey man, look at what a church gave us kitchen people. They came in with some bags of vegetables and crackers, but a lady told me to take this to us all back here. Just for us." He opened up a box of chocolate turtles, a caramel-and-nut confection that was a favorite of mine as a kid.

"Man, I haven't seen these in years," said Carl, holding one up, turning it over and admiring it.

"Huh. Me neither," said Russ.

"Now, that's the most words you'll get out of ol' Russ all day," laughed Herbie, handing out the candies. "So I know he must be excited. Eat up, everybody."

Carl launched back into his talk about school while he nibbled on the chocolate coating. As I bit hard into the chocolate caramel and nut candy, I felt an immediate stab of lightning streak through my jaw line. I yelped in pain.

"What's the matter, Brad-man?" asked Herbie.

I brought my hand up to my mouth and spit out two halves of a tooth. Biting down on the candy had shattered one of my side teeth.

"Ooooh," said Carl, "nasty. You busted it clean out, man. You got weak teeth. Don't you have a dentist who takes care of you so you don't have no weak teeth?"

"No," I answered, spitting out blood. "Never could afford one."

"Well, how 'bout that," said Herbie, grinning and showing a missing front tooth. "Brad-man's one of us."

I smiled and spit out some more blood. Part of the guys, huh?

After we served the meals in the large dining hall, Ben came over. "You gonna teach us tonight?"

"Yessir," I said. "I have a study on praise to God."

Ben nodded and pulled a cigarette out of a pack. "Good, good, we want something deep. And you'll like the Man's singing tonight. Got a good voice, he does."

Andy, one of the staff, walked outside and threw a bag of garbage into the dumpster. A stocky dark-bearded man who wore a red jumpsuit every day that I was there, Andy was now clean and sober for over four months. He was happy to be free of those habits that nearly took away his life at the young age of twenty-two. One habit, however, that he still battled was that of gossip. Andy loved the small universe of the rescue mission, but his affection grew into a busybody attitude that was quickly getting on everybody's nerves.

I was in the back, sitting on a crate and preparing for the Bible study out near the vegetable boxes while Ben sat on an upside-down trash can and smoked quietly. Andy strolled out and leaned against the wall.

He looked at Ben. "Did you hear about Steve, and how he's been trying to sneak a drink again? And he's a trustee, too," he said.

Ben looked up and breathed a long sentence. "Therebutgodgome."

Andy paused and looked at him for a moment. He slowly continued. "Steve's been given the keys to handle the food pantry, but now he's been walking across the street and looking over the vodka at the package store. He even told a fellow that he might try some late at night."

Ben took a puff and looked at the sky. "Therebutgodgome."

Andy shook his head slightly. I was puzzled as well. I couldn't make out Ben's mumbling.

Andy continued. "And I think that Steve might be talking too much with Wanda, the woman's trustee over in a place called The Shelter. They say he's spending a little more time than he should. Might be flirting."

Ben tapped the ash on the ground. "Therebutgodgome."

Andy shrugged. "I – I don't get what you're saying. I don't understand. What is it you're saying?"

Ben turned and enunciated slowly: "*There but God go me.* Look, son, I'm not gonna sit here and talk about someone else, because but for the grace of God, I'd be doing the same thing. Hey, instead of talking *about* Steve, why don't you try to go talk *to* him? Seems the Jesus way to do things."

"Yeah, but I'm white and he's black," argued Andy. "He won't listen to me if I try to correct him."

"God ain't got no color, man," said Ben.

Andy stared at Ben and considered this. Without saying a word, he nodded his head and walked quietly inside. That was the last time I heard Andy gossip about anyone. Whether he talked with Steve or not, I don't know. I do know, however, that he was taught a very powerful lesson that night.

A tall man came wandering out and sat near us. He looked out around the parking lot, not saying a word. "You doin' okay, buddy?" I asked. He didn't respond at all. After a minute, he walked inside.

"He's new here," said Ben. "Walkin' the railroad line for quite some time."

"Really? How would you know?"

Ben turned to me. "He's a white fellow, right? When he stumbled in here this afternoon, he had so much grease and tar from railroad ties and sleeping in puddles of oil along the tracks, he was blacker than me." He dropped his cigarette on the ground and stepped on it. "His clothes were so full of lice we had to burn them. Ran him through the showers for forty minutes until we started seein' his real color." He looked at me. "Some of them coming in here are bad, Brad-man. *Real* bad. That's what makes helping out here so important to me. Gotta help those who are down so hard."

The evening's service was held in the dining hall, and the room was fairly full.

Ben was right. Ed's tenor voice was so engaging that we hung on every note as he sang song after song. He was a gifted guitarist as well, and led he whole room in chorus singing that brought tears to my eyes. There was no pretense in this room, no desire to put on airs. When "Amazing Grace" was sung, you knew that every word held a deep significance.

Amazing grace! How sweet the sound

That saved a wretch like me.

I once was lost, but now am found.

Was blind, but now I see.

Once again, I walked up to the battered music stand that would serve as my podium. I was wearing jeans and a polo shirt, the attire recommended by Ed. I looked about and asked everyone to bow their heads so that we could start in prayer.

I looked down to the row right in front of me. There sat Ronald. He refused to look at me – and he would not look my way through the entire message - but he was filing page after page with notes while he turned to each Bible reference.

I asked Ed to lead us in prayer. He stood up, humbled, and bowed his head. Men and women around him murmured their support and approval as he spoke.

"Dearest heavenly Father who lives above and is worthy of our praise..." *Yes, Lord, you are worthy*, the voices said.

"You have given us life when we didn't deserve it and You shower us with blessings even when we fail You." *Yes, it's true, Lord, You're good even when we're not.*

"I am humbled, Lord, with the fact that You let us pray to You. I'm a sinner, but You are forgiving." *Yes, Lord, good gracious, yes.*

"Please make this a special time tonight, Father. We need You and we need Your Word." *Yes, Lord we need it.*

"Please give Brad the words to say." *Yes, Lord, give Him the words.*

"Don't let him speak his own words. Shut him up if he tries to speak on his own." *Yes, Lord, shut him up.*

"In Jesus' heavenly, holy name we pray, Amen." *Amen.*

Carl stood up and called out. "I asked Brad-man to give us some of those Hebrew words, the ones you find in the Old Testament."

Herbie popped up. "And I wanted to know more about singing and prayer stuff. He promised that, too." He looked at me. "Sorry for yelling."

I laughed and bobbed my head. "I think that we can handle both of those tonight."

"All right, then. Bring it," said Steve.

I looked out across the room and began with a story. "I heard about a newspaper reporter who, years ago, had a chance to interview a well-known symphony orchestra conductor from Eastern Europe. This conductor had been released from a prison sentence because his political views didn't match up with his government, and they threw him in jail for almost a decade. Worse yet, they threw him in solitary confinement, and he couldn't talk with anyone. But now he was free."

"The newspaper reporter asked the famous maestro, 'Sir, when you were thrown into solitary confinement and could have no music to hear, what music would you have considered then as the most beautiful?'"

"'The most beautiful?' the maestro asked. 'Yes, sir,' the reporter answered. 'Ah, my friend,' the maestro said, with a tear rolling down his cheek, 'the most beautiful music I wanted to hear was the sound of a voice of kindness.'"

"Ah, ah, ah. Isn't that the truth," said Ben aloud, his voice cracking with emotion.

I continued. "May we remember that there are those around us that simply want the beauty of a Christian's voice of caring. That really is the most beautiful music to a thirsty soul."

"Yes," said Carl. "Amen to *that*."

I held up my Bible.

"We *crave* kindness. We love it when we are the recipients of an act of care. And you know? Our Heavenly Father is ready to give us loving care and kindness every day. Every day! Look with me in Psalm 136. This passage is known to the Jews as the Great Hallel."

"He's going with the Hebrew words, just like I asked," said Ben.

I read: "*Give thanks to the LORD, for He is good, for His lovingkindness is everlasting. Give thanks to the God of gods, for His lovingkindness is everlasting.*"

"You see, the entire passage of Psalm 136 is like one big gigantic shout of praise, 'Hallel.' We shout thank you to God for His kindness! How do we shout? Think of that word 'Hallel.' It has a very powerful history."

"Here we go," said Ben. "Watch out, now."

"I'm writing this down," called Herbie.

"Shhhh," said Ed.

I smiled and continued. "We go into a meeting and sing praises, right? Well, you might go into any meeting and hear one of two kinds of praise. We should always praise Him, you know. In fact, the Hebrew name for 'Psalms' is *tehillim* and it means 'praises.' It is from the root word *halal*, meaning 'to make a jubilant sound' that's supposed to be aimed at God and all He does. If a worshiper uses this kind of praise, he is rejoicing *directly at the Almighty*. And that's only right, because of how He's lifted us up. That's one kind of *halal*, a praise that goes overboard in thanking God for the lovingkindness He's shown."

I raised my finger.

"However, there is another meaning for **halal**. It can also mean 'to praise or boast of one's self' so much that you become foolish. In other words, you're praising all right, but you're praising yourself, because you want attention pointed at you."

"Selfish," called a woman.

"Bring it," said Carl.

I looked around the room. "Which means you can make one of two choices whenever you come to a praise service..."

"Tell us," said Ben.

I said, "You can be Godly in your praise and 'be a fool for God' ... or you can be *just plain foolish* – stupid, really - if you decide to praise yourself! The big question is, who gets the attention when you start singing in a service? God lets you make your choice. Him or you?"

Ed clapped and laughed. "Let it always be Him!"

Herbie shook his head and Carl shouted. "I'm with Ed. God did the work – God gets the praise!"

I looked down. Ronald was looking away from me, but I caught a brief smile.

Ed came back up front, and oh, did we have a praise time that night.

But as they say, all good things must come to an end. Soon it was the end of two weeks at Red Street. My heart was heavy on the final night at the rescue mission. It was past midnight and we were still sitting on the front bench of the property, behind a fence (they locked the gates at night, not to keep us in, but to protect us from the high crime in the area. This part of Oakland was said to be the most violent in all the city.)

I had been sitting in the midst of five men who had been asking questions on every conceivable Bible subject.

"Did Nicodemus ever become a Christian?"

"Is it wrong to ever get angry? What does the Bible say?"

"That stuff in Ezekiel that I read last week – is that about flying saucers?"

153

"So how long is eternity?"

In the midnight hour the only thing illuminated was a nearby streetlight and the orange ends of the cigarettes of the men as they smoked and talked.

As we sat there, I looked across the road at the package store. We could see a figure climbing in the side window.

"So, preacher," Andy said, "how long was Jesus on the cross?"

"Um, guys," I said, pointing. "There's someone breaking into that store right across the street."

"Happens all the time," said Steve. "Silent alarm will get 'em. You'd think the word would get around. Say, what's this rapture thing all about, preacher?"

Sure enough, as we talked, the police slid up to a stop, jumped out and corralled the burglar. He was handcuffed and whisked off within a few minutes.

Carl looked at me. "They try this about three times a week. They always get caught." He spit on the ground. "Stupid."

A sharp banging and a loud shout came from within the building. "What's that?" I asked, turning to see a light come on in the side hallway.

"Not good, Brad-man, not good," said Herbie as he trotted outside in his pajamas. "A guy in there has been swearing, thrashing and kicking in his bunk bed, says he's gonna kill someone and the other guys are yelling for him to shut up."

"What do you mean?" asked Andy.

Ben walked over with an explanation. "We have a fellow who's been making a racket and it's about to start a fight inside. He's got himself dressed and is demanding that Ed unlock the gate and let him leave. Of course, the Mission has to let him go. We're not allowed to hold anyone against their will."

"Well, that's good, isn't it?" I asked. "He needs to blow off some steam..."

"Well, Brad-man, let me explain the whole story," said Ben, sitting down on the bench. "This guy's name is John, and he's a serviceman who just came back from overseas, Egypt or Honduras, I'm not sure which. He's a small fella with little-boy freckles, not very tall or very big. He was married and moved into an apartment just about a month before he went over. Well, he served his duty, but in the last few months before his time was up, he couldn't get his new wife to respond to his mail and couldn't get her to phone him or make contact."

Ben leaned back. "Well, yesterday he got back to the States. Today when he arrived in Oakland, he got to his apartment and found his wife there – with another man who had moved in and taken over. Tall, big guy, and here's John, this little fella. His wife, she's there making fun of him, saying she got a better man and if he didn't like it, why doesn't he do something about it. That big fella moved in and took over all of John's stuff – his tools, his furniture, everything. So not only has John lost his wife, he's got nothing. He'd even been sending his checks home to her, and they'd both been spending them all. The guy's only choice was to come here tonight."

"But he's got rage, preacher," said Herbie.

"Oh, yeah," nodded Ben. "Lots of rage. He's been thrashing in there, saying that he's going to go back and torch them both, kill them. He was making so much noise that the whole dorm room was ready to break out in a fight. He's got his clothes on and he's coming out. Preacher, he's gonna go kill them tonight."

"Wait. Can't the police do something?" I asked.

Carl shrugged. "Oakland Police won't do anything unless a crime has been committed. They're not there to stop something before it's happened."

John burst out of the side door and marched toward the gate.

"John, this here's the preacher," Ben said, pointing at me. "Look, just talk to him before we unlock the gates, okay?"

John stopped and looked at me. Even in the darkness, I could see him quaking in rage.

"John, you've been treated wrong, but you don't want to do this," I said.

"Preacher, I know that God is the final judge, but there's just some things a man has gotta do," said John, looking at the gate. "I'm gonna get me some gas and some flame and do some justice tonight."

"But John, what then?" I asked. "You'll do jail time? Look, you think you've lost everything, but you haven't."

He shook his head. "No disrespect, but telling me I still have God just ain't going to cut it right now, you know?"

Carl came over. "You got friends here now, man. We ain't much, but we can help. We got God on our side."

"Yeah," Herbie reached out, unsure of whether to pat John. He settled for a wave. "Hey, most of us got shafted somehow."

I was searching for the right words to say. "John, I'm not going to try to shove Bible verses at you, or try to act like I know what you're going through, but I do know that if you stay here we can do what we can to get you on your feet, and I can tell you how you can find a way to forgive. God'll make a way, but you've got to give it some time."

Ben stepped closer. "We can help you work through it, all of us."

John snorted and shook his head. "Yeah, well, it'll take all of you to be able to teach me about forgiveness. You think you can do that?"

"Yeah, we can," came a voice from behind him. A man stepped into the streetlight. It was Ronald.

He looked at John and patted him on the shoulder. "Yeah, man, no matter how bad it gets, God can help. Take it from me." Then he turned and looked me in the eye.

"And you can call me Ron."

9.

Oregon: the Wedding Singer, the Flirt, and the Clockmaker

I traveled the final few northern miles on California's Interstate 5 and glanced over at the "Welcome to Oregon" sign. I was going to be taking a break from speaking for a few days while in Medford.

Chico, California had been a week of unpredictable events with Scotty Hellwege, a college and career pastor who was a former classmate of mine. Scotty was one of the crazy guys in our hall, a fellow who made the Dean's List every term and yet gave you the distinct feeling that he never really matured beyond the ninth grade. He was the guy who was sliding down the dorm's stairwell on cardboard sleds, stuffing two baked potatoes in his mouth without chewing, or driving his car in reverse through the Wendy's drive-thru.

Now Scotty was married to a wonderful girl named Debbie and had a strong young adult ministry in California. Now *this* I wanted to see. Had he grown up?

I was invited to stay at Scotty and Deb's home, enjoying their guest bedroom and Deb's home-cooked meals. The meetings were, well, *fun*. The church had a unique speaking presentation; Scotty and I would team up each evening and divide the message in half. Scotty would speak first for twenty minutes and then I would conclude the message with my "half" of the sermon for another twenty minutes. Although I was hesitant at the possibility that this might be seen as showboating, it actually was a case of "iron sharpening iron," as we worked hard to meet each other's goals of a thorough Bible presentation. Those attending told me that they found it a refreshing approach to preaching the Bible, seeing it through two different perspectives each night. We spoke on topics such as the "Holiness of God", "Why is There Suffering in the World?" and "How We Can Make Our Neighborhood and Workplace an Active Mission Field." There were many good responses to the messages, and I enjoyed it immensely. Even though I had been put in numerous different speaking situations – once while standing on a bunk bed in a dormitory, another over a CB channel to truckers on a Sunday morning - this two-speaker presentation was a new one to me.

But oh, Scotty and I barely kept out of trouble.

On the first day trouble was at hand at his Sunday afternoon backyard barbecue. For some reason neither Scotty nor Deb changed from their Sunday finery into, well, picnic clothes. I saw disaster in the waiting as Deb moved about in a pale pink chiffon dress handling condiments and foodstuffs. It wasn't Deb's coordination I was worried about; you guessed it – it was Scotty's. Sure enough, as he was rambling on about a Halloween prank he'd heard, he picked up the KC Masterpiece Barbecue sauce and shook it vigorously before he poured it over the ribs.

You guessed it. The cap wasn't on.

Deb was right behind him.

The result was that Deb looked like the final scene in the movie *Bonnie and Clyde*. She had deep brownish-red spots riddled all over her dress and face. As if that wasn't bad enough, Scotty turned around and burst out laughing, with no compassion whatsoever. Worse yet, for reasons unknown to me, he began pointing to me and encouraging me to yuck it up as well.

Murder had never been so seriously contemplated by the wife of a pastor. Double murder, in fact, and yet I sat there dumbfounded - I don't know how I was being blamed, except by association.

The rest of the week wasn't any easier. He and I visited a nursing home and he insisted on retrieving both of an elderly woman resident's slippers so she could attend the Bible study, only to have her shut him up long enough to let him know that she was an amputee; she only had one foot.

Then he insisted on keeping a stray kitten in his car, thinking it cute to have it wander around the car's interior as we made visits around the city. It was all well and fun until we got to a busy intersection and due to a construction project, he was forced to slam on his brakes and change lanes. Except he couldn't, because the kitten had crawled down to the floorboards and fallen asleep - *under* the brake pedal. Only quick NASCAR-like moves prevented us from a serious accident.

On Tuesday his basement flooded because he forgot to turn off the bathroom sink faucet before the service. On Wednesday his front seat smelled like vinegar because he tried unsuccessfully to balance an Italian tureen on the front seat with only his hand, resulting in a gooey, noodly mess. The back of his car smelled like rotten garbage because he had thrown three hefty bags full of moldy-food trash in the trunk - and forgot about it for four days, the last day of my visit.

And somehow it kept looking like I brought the problems on.

I left Chico safely enough, but I will always remember Deb's eye twitching uncontrollably as I pulled out of the driveway. For the next year I was careful not to open any UPS packages from the Chico area. You never know what Deb would try for revenge.

Now on to Oregon. I had been asked by an old friend, Trixie Vaughn, if I might officiate her wedding, and since I was on the West Coast during that time of the year, I gladly accepted. I'd always liked the Vaughn family since I was a kid, and it was going to be an extra special weekend in catching up on all the news since they moved from the East.

The reunion with the family was everything I expected. They had moved out onto a nice little farm and escorted me over to a second building - a trailer they had made for visiting missionaries who needed some privacy during their furloughs. It was ornate, done in a theme that had a rural Oregonian flavor. Plus, there was a big bowl of fruit on the counter.

I sat down with the family and we talked over old times back on the Eastern Shore - the pig roasts on the church's Old Fashioned Day, the Fireman's carnivals, and the 4-H fairs they so dearly loved. We went late into the night.

"Better head to bed, son," said Larry, the father said to me. "The rehearsal's tomorrow, and I want to show you around the area before then."

"Come on," said Todd, "I'll take you back out to the Missionary House." He led me out to the trailer, gave me a key, and said good night.

I sunk into the bed within fifteen minutes and was sound asleep. However, deep into the morning hours I was awakened by a roaring headache. My temples were throbbing and my eyes were pounding. I sat up, groaning aloud. I had experienced migraines all through my youth, but those were mostly from sinuses, and were located in specific regions of my head. This was all-encompassing, coursing through my whole skull. I stumbled into the small kitchen area and took a drink. I immediately started sweating profusely. The room - no, the entire trailer felt stifling. In the wee hours of the morning, I pushed my way outside and fell into the grass. The water wasn't sitting well in my stomach. I vomited numerous times. Did I have a fever?

My commotion caught the attention of the Vaughn bedrooms nearest the trailer. Someone threw open a window. "Are you okay, Brad?"

"My head... killing me," I mumbled. I could hardly speak, I was in such pain. Lights came on inside the house and I felt hands lift me up and help me walk into the house. I was given a room with the other boys and after some hours and a few Tylenol, I slowly felt the ripping pain ebb out of my temples.

The next morning I shuffled into the kitchen, rubbing my face. The whole family looked at me with a collective concerned expression.

"How are you feeling, hon?" asked Penny, the mother.

"Exhausted. I don't think I have the flu, though," I replied, feeling my forehead."

Larry shook his head and put down his cup of coffee. "No, son, it wasn't the flu." He was having a hard time looking at me.

I pulled up a chair and plopped down. "What do you think I picked up? Not food poisoning?" I looked at Penny. "No offense intended." Boy, *that* didn't come out right.

"Nope," said Larry, finally meeting my eyes. "The boys and I searched every corner of the trailer, and we found what I suspected. There was a serious gas leak in there." He picked up his cup and looked over the rim at me. "Perhaps you'd better stay in the house on one of the bunk beds."

This was the day of the practice, and Trixie flitted about the church, carrying candles, napkins, doilies, and swatches of clothing. In fact, virtually every female was darting about the church in some sort of preparatory activity. I was to be the minister presenting the vows, and I was to go over the order of service with Trixie and Paul, her husband-to-be. Everyone was now being given explicit instructions as to their placement and their part of the ceremony. Penny was giving instructions down to the last detail, and everyone was following it closely – except one person.

During the rehearsal walk-through as I was jotting down notes, I couldn't help but notice a stocky long-haired young lady with a cowgirl swagger, parading before everyone else and totally oblivious to the need to listen to her specific order during the practice. Her arrogance was beyond irritating; it was actually fascinating. She was openly trying to catch everyone's attention, but I couldn't figure out why. I was told that she was a friend of Trixie's, and she was going to sing a solo during the wedding service.

Everything in the rehearsal went off without a hitch, if you excluded Cowgirl's inattention.

The next day friends and family packed the auditorium for the wedding. Everyone was looking grand in their finery, especially the wedding party. The elderly piano player was giving a fine rendition of numerous compositions by Brahms, and the many flower displays gave a soft genteel look to the room. I checked the program as I stood before the auditorium audience. The violins had just finished playing, and now it was time for the Cowgirl's song. All was quiet as the young lady strutted to the front, grabbed a microphone and looked above the crowd in as serene a profile as she could muster. Her accompanist, who had nudged the elderly lady off of the piano bench, played the opening chords. Then I realized that this would be trouble. The girl had not practiced last night, but the way she held the microphone, I knew we were all in trouble.

She was treating the mike as if it were concert quality. She was holding it a mere inch from her mouth and I saw her swell up to bellow out her first notes, but I knew from last night's practice that this was a small-potatoes public address system, only made for simple speaking and narrations; the electronic speakers had a limit.

It was too late to do anything. I winced at what was coming.

It came.

She wound up and belted out he first words.

So many nights I sit by my window

Waiting for someone...

My gut turned. She was singing her own rendition of "You Light Up My Life," but not in the lilting gentle romantic way it was suppose to be sung. She was making it more along the lines of Ethel Merman in *Annie Get Your Gun*.

It was loud. She punched every word.

And You! Light! Up! My! Life!

You! Give! Me! Hope!

I saw Paul gritting his teeth. I believe a gentleman in the back lost his toupee. I mean, the windows were rattling during this song.

She hit the last notes – *You light up my LIIIIIIIFE* - and I believe I heard a dog howl in a nearby neighborhood. But the best part was to come.

As she finished, she slammed the microphone back into its holder and looked at the crowd in expectation.

And I saw her face fall. *Then I knew.* As I looked at her shocked expression, I realized that she fully expected a standing ovation, or at least full-throated cheering. Instead, she got silence.

As she stomped back to her seat, I became aware of the glaring fact that this girl forgot all about the wedding; *she thought the whole ceremony was about her.*

And, believe it or not, during that little part of the ceremony, I got another life lesson on the road that would impact my approach to the ministry.

Many times we go to church to be seen, not to seek. On a weekly basis we tend to forget the all-time truth: **Praise goes to God and God alone.** It got me to thinking about many of the nation's churches and the rut into which they'd fallen. The church pleases God not when it makes itself marketable or socially exciting, but when it shows man how to put himself in humility and submission in order to properly praise God. Moreover, God wants a deep family-love from His people and wishes to display His love for anyone who would receive it. And Christians who just look at themselves aren't very loveable family members.

God wants to be discovered, but you have to be willing to do the searching. Realize, though, that *He* is the object of our worship. Not our church, not our social life, not our friends, not even our music. It's Him and only Him.

I'm reminded of Psalm 150 and the emphasis upon God, not us:

*Praise the LORD; Praise God in his sanctuary; praise **Him** in his mighty firmament. Praise **Him** for his mighty deeds; praise **Him** according to his surpassing greatness. Praise **Him** with trumpet sound; praise **Him** with lute and harp. Praise **Him** with tambourine and dance; praise **Him** with strings and pipe. Praise **Him** with clanging cymbals; praise **Him** with loud clashing cymbals. Let everything that breathes praise the LORD. Praise the LORD (RSV)*

The above Psalm - the final thought of all the Psalms - reminds us that **it is not about us.**

After the wedding I swung back south into California and to the community of Lakeport, California. The Golden State Church had asked me to speak for a week, and I immediately fell in love with the whole body of believers, especially the pastor and his wife. The McConnells were a genuine couple; there was nothing showy nor pretentious about them in the least. They were a young couple in a church whose average age was sixty. This made no difficulty at all; in fact, the relationship between the pastor's family and the congregation was one of the most intimate that I'd ever seen. When Mrs. McConnell gave birth to their first child, I realized that this new family would never, ever need to pay for babysitting services; they had over sixty pairs of grandparents who would fight over the right to care for the newborn.

Speaking at a church of retirees was new to me. Most of my speaking engagements and ministry services had been to youth groups, school chapels and college organizations. The pastor and his wife were the youngest people in the church by at least thirty years. I was by far the youngest whippersnapper in the place, and here I was, the speaker for the week.

The first challenge this presented to me was that I was the object of outrageous flirtation - by every woman over seventy-five. In fact, at a small luncheon with the pastor, his wife and two ladies, I detected an acrimonious spirit between the widowed Mrs. Spenser and the widowed Mrs. Hancock. Mrs. Spenser, at eighty-four the eldest of the two by at least ten years, plied me with questions throughout the meal, covering such wide-ranging subjects such as my family upbringing to my view on Reagan's dealing with the Soviets. The meal was sumptuous and everyone was in an expansive mood as we walked out of the restaurant – everyone, that is, except the driver of our car, Mrs. Hancock.

As we all got into our seats we heard the distinctively clear comment from the driver's seat: "Well, I would have had a good time, but you took up all the conversation with the young man." The pastor glanced at me and Mrs. McConnell looked away, trying not to smile. I could see Mrs. Spenser trying to ease the situation by throwing gentle questions toward Mrs. Spenser, but she was having none of it. She was *mad*, brother, and she was plotting to do something about it. I wasn't sure how I felt about being in the middle of a tempestuous relationship such as this, for never had anyone actually fought for my attention. With the age difference I couldn't see any future in a possible relationship, so I wasn't sure if this was flattering. The McConnells were dropped off at their home across town, and now it was me sitting in the back seat, looking at the very tense white-haired scalps of the two competing ladies. I could tell something was going on in Mrs. Hancock's head – she was looking for revenge of some kind. She finally found it:

"Say, I have a neighborhood where everyone grows rose bushes in their front yard. I want to show them to you, young man."

Mrs. Spenser looked over at her. "That's a nice idea, Edna. I'd like to see them myself."

Mrs. Spenser had her ace and she played it with the fervor of a cowhand with a winning hand at a poker table. "Oh, not *you*. I'm dropping you off. It's just the young man and me."

Before I could say anything, she pulled the car up to the curb in front of the Spenser mailbox.

"Uh," said Mrs. Spenser.

"Here you go," said Mrs. Hancock breezily. "See you tonight at church." As Mrs. Spenser pulled herself from the car, it almost seemed as if she were mentally cursing herself. Her face was in open anguish, but she had no choice. She shut the car door and shuffled towards her front step. As we swung around I could see her looking our way.

"And here we are," said Mrs. Spenser pointing and driving happily, puttering along at two miles per hour. "These are called 'Rosa Californica' bushes, and they're native to the state... oh, and those are called China Roses, aren't they pretty?" She pulled up to the next property. "These are called tea roses... I don't know what those are across the street, but aren't they a nice yellow?" She did a U-turn. "And these are my very own red roses. I made a nice long line of them. Okay, did you like that?" She punched the gas and took me back to the McConnell house where I was staying. The whole Jealousy Rose tour took all of ninety seconds.

What was it with me and women who were fifty years my senior? I could never figure out my attraction.

On the fourth day of the meetings, Pastor McConnell pulled me into his office. He offered me a seat and settled himself quietly behind his desk. "Each night, as you know, we've had a family take care of your evening meal. I had people sign up weeks ago, not only because it gives them a chance to share in the giving part of ministry, but it also gives them a chance to get to know you, our speaker, better."

I nodded. "Yes, Pastor, and I appreciate it. The conversations have been even better than the food. Each family has a great history, and they're all superb storytellers. Each dinner is like reading a book," I said.

He blanched a bit. "Mmm. Good. Uh, like I said, I had people sign up ahead of time..." He paused and tapped a pencil on the desk.

"Yes?" I didn't feel comfortable with his pause.

"... and I feel committed to honor all of those sign-ups..." He looked down at his desk.

I shrugged. "Is this about the people who signed up for tonight?"

"Yes," said the pastor, looking at me. "Rather, it's the one person who signed up to give you dinner."

I waited.

"His name is Granville Yates." He blinked. "You know who I'm talking about."

I swallowed. Yes, I did.

Granville Yates was, to say the least, an eccentric. A seventy-year-old bachelor, Yates sported an Albert Einstein-inspired uncombed look and wore clothes that were at least two sizes too big for him. Each night of the meetings he lugged in a boombox and sat in the exact middle of the congregation. He loved my sermons and told everyone that he was going to record my messages for his future study. However, that meant that Mr. Yates punched his boom box's button to "record" from where he sat, trusting that my voice would come in clear and crisp despite the people coughing, air conditioning adjusting and other ambient noises that permeate the average church auditorium.

There was another problem with his recording scheme. His audio cassette tape was only fifteen minutes per side, meaning he would hear the "click" of the tape, switch it over, and punch "record" again. This in itself would be no problem, except that Mr. Yates fell asleep in each of my messages. Every one. The "click" would startle him awake, whereby he would panic and rewind the tape in confusion. He would then fumble around, trying to figure out where I had finished my last phrase so that he'd have a smooth transition as he turned over the tape, and he would turn up the volume to get an idea of where the tape had stopped recording. He would mistakenly crank the volume up to a full blast and turn on the tape - remember, this was right in the middle of my message – and fiddle around with the buttons until he was able to change sides. Few things would confuse me during my speaking engagements as much as hearing my own voice shouting at me at a supersonic level in the middle of my own sermon. The added feature to all this was that it scared the ever-lovin' wits out of everybody within five rows in any direction. Due to the age of the congregation I seriously considered asking the pastor to have a paramedic on hand each evening. This happened every night.

This was the man who was taking me to dinner.

"I've, er, talked with him about cooking you a meal," said the pastor, "and told him he was not allowed to do that." I didn't even want to begin trying to figure out what *that* meant. "In fact, Brad, you can back out if you want to."

I raised my hands. "Pastor, how can I do that? He's made a commitment to show a generosity to me. I can't turn away from that, can I?" I leaned forward. *"Can* I?"

Pastor McConnell only said, "I think it'll be okay as long as he's taking you out to a restaurant."

So I agreed to go.

Within an hour, Granville Yates stopped by and gave me the details. "I'll be picking you up in front of the church here at four o'clock. I'll be taking you to a nice diner – I can't really cook, so I don't want you to eat at my home." He grinned. "There's another reason for us going to the diner. There's been a waitress that I've known for over a year there – Brenda's her name - and I've been trying to talk to her about heaven. She says she's not a Christian, so if we go eat there, then I'll open up the conversation for you and you can take care of it!"

I've always been uneasy when people use me as sort of a magic genie, wanting me to wave my hands and produce a miracle in one short meeting. This had happened a couple of times during my circuit, and I learned to have sympathy for pastors who are thrown innocently into a meeting – often through a ruse – so that a person can corner another family member can have the opportunity to see the minister "sic 'em."

He actually cackled. "We got her now!"

I sighed, but told Mr. Yates that I would try my best. In the middle of this woman's working hours in serving tables and earn tip money, I was supposed to try to stop her and give her the plan of salvation... well, he *did* say he'd "set it up."

He picked me up in a rusty yellow VW Beetle at precisely four o'clock, bubbling with excitement. "You'll like this place," he gushed. "It's got a great menu – all kinds of dishes, you can try anything you want. And we also get to catch Brenda so you can talk with her!" He laughed aloud.

We pulled up to a ramshackle clapboard restaurant that best fits the description "greasy spoon." The place looked like the owners made a recent decision to change from a hay barn to a sit-down restaurant. None of the chairs matched, and the uneven floor had dirty wood planking. Mr. Yates handed me a wrinkled menu. "Try anything."

I looked it over and the only safe thing seemed to be a plate of French fries. I mean, the oil would be hot enough to burn off any diseases, right?

"Here she comes, here she comes," snickered Granville Yates. "She has to take our order, and when she does, I'll introduce you and, you know, set it up."

"Okay, Mr. Yates." I started to take a drink from my water glass but decided against it. The rim had lipstick on it.

Brenda came over, harried and yet cheerful. She was middle-aged but energetic, and it was obvious that she was overworked. She had been waiting on four others tables, carrying plates of food. "Hey, Brenda, gal," said Mr. Yates.

"An' how're you doing?" responded Brenda in a husky but upbeat voice. I was fairly certain that she didn't really know Mr. Yates as well as he made it out to be.

"Well," he said expansively, "I'll have the scrambled eggs with biscuits. And a sausage. Oh, and a glass of milk." He slapped down his menu and pointed at me. "And I'm paying for his meal."

"How nice," said Brenda.

"Uh, I'll have a hamburger, please," I said.

"Coke or Sprite?"

"No, thank you, this water's fine."

"Okay, then." She picked up the paper menus. Granville turned and winked at me. Here was his big opening.

"Brenda," he said loudly. She turned to face him.

He leaned his face to within a foot of hers. *"How's your rotten ol' soul?"*

She stared at him with blank eyes and one of her eyelids flickered. She stuck out her chin and said, "It's gettin' *rottener*." And she turned and headed into the kitchen.

An expression flickered across his face, and I could tell that he was reconsidering whether this was an appropriate line with which to start a conversation about salvation. His eyes grew troubled, and when she had another waitress deliver our food, I was sure he decided that he'd made a mistake. Her name never came up again.

After our prayer, he slurped down everything in front of him – milk, sausage, eggs - before I was even halfway through the hamburger. "Come on," he said, wiping his mouth on the back of his sleeve. "We have time before the service tonight. I want to take you to my home. I have something to give you."

I left Brenda as nice a tip as I could, squeezed back into his Beetle and we puttered across town to an older section of Lakeport. "I've lived here all of my life," he said, "and at one time my business was one of the top companies in town." He swung into a pothole-filled side street and entered the first driveway on the right. This was his property. We pulled into a carport-type of construction that was leaning at such an angle that I wondered whether slamming the car door would topple the wooden barn. Decrepit was an apt word to describe the structure.

"Come on, we'll take the back way," said Mr. Yates. He motioned for me to come around to the back gate; it hung on one hinge, swinging crazily. "Should... should I shut it?" I asked, immediately realizing how inane that sounded.

"Yes, better make sure it's shut," he said, walking through waist high weeds in the back yard. As I followed him my feet felt something concrete; there was actually a sidewalk path underneath all of this growth.

We climbed the back steps of an unpainted two-story house. I searched for something to say as I stood at the top of the staircase. Three steps were missing. "Uh, this sure gives you a nice view of the ...neighborhood," I tried.

"Yeah, I've always felt that it's the best view on this street. Come in this way." He held open the screen door for me and I entered through what might be called the utility room. A large sink and faucet were located on the left-hand side of this back porch. Hundreds of empty fly-infested tuna cans reached a full two feet above the rim of the sink. "My kittens love tuna," he offered.

"Yes, I can see," I said. I followed Mr. Yates into the back room, which was his kitchen. The room was poorly lit, the linoleum was curled and greasy, and the refrigerator looked to be from the mid-1950s era. He pulled open the fridge with a jerk and brought out a carton of orange juice. The opening was crusty and flaked with dark brown flecks. He popped it open. "Those eggs made me extra thirsty," he said, gulping furiously. He turned to me and held out the carton. "Would you like a drink?"

I stepped back as quickly and yet as politely as I could. "Well, no thank you, I've pretty well had my fill of water ... er, I'm fine." He shrugged and stuffed it back inside the refrigerator.

"Hey, come on in here. I have something to give you, preacher."

I stepped into the next room and stared. I was looking at two things in as great a quantity as I'd ever seen in my life. First, there were cats everywhere. Dozens of them wandering around, meowing contentedly and playing happily. They were on the lampstand. They curled on top of the old television set and the nearby sofa. They played with the curtains. They wandered over to me and rubbed against my leg, purring.

Second, the walls were literally covered with clocks. *Covered* with them. Kitchen clocks, antique clocks, cuckoo clocks, chiming clocks, cat-with-moving-tail-and-eyes-clocks... they took up every available inch of wallpaper space in this room and the rooms beyond. It was fascinating and a bit eerie.

"I used to be in the clock repair business," he said proudly. "Everybody in town would bring me their watches and clocks to fix."

Out of the corner of my eye I saw a cat continually walk in a circular pattern. She was obviously trying to get my attention but she couldn't break that pattern of walking in the same circle. I pointed this out to Mr. Yates.

"Oh, her," he said. "She was walking under a clock and it fell on her head. That was about a year ago. Hit her pretty hard. She's been walking in circles ever since. Poor kitty." He waved his hand. "I have something for you."

He darted into a room and I reached down to pet the little orbital cat. I shook my head. Some days are filled with the most unpredictable things...

He came out of the room with a huge grin. "I want you to have this."

175

I nodded, smiling but wondering. Was this like the stories played out on those late-night movies? An old eccentric man gives a treasure to a struggling youngster to help him on his way? *It just might be the Lord's doing.* I had seventeen dollars in my pocket and at the end of this week I was due to be in Denver, Colorado. Just maybe...

He tucked a large flat envelope in my hand. I opened it up. It was a 1964 cartoon tourism map of the town. There were grease marks on each of the corners.

"This is something for you to remember us by," he said happily.

I stared at it and realized that this was bringing the joy of giving to an old man who just waned to help a ministry in the best way he knew how. I was touched. I really was. "Thank you. I'll always keep this," I said to him. And I have.

I tucked the map into my coat pocket and waved my arms around. "Mr. Yates, did you retire from clock making? I mean, you have so much inventory here."

"Well, I stopped my business years ago because of the deadlines. There was so much to do that I started getting sick, real sick, in the head." He looked at the clocks. "So, I closed for business to the folks in town, because people were yelling about getting their clocks fixed in a hurry. But then that made me sad, because I do love my clock repairing as much as my kittens. I went to church and told the people how sad I was because I was confused. I couldn't stand for people to yell at me to hurry and fix their clocks, but I still like to repair them."

"And you know what?" He looked at me and threw his hands wide. "Suddenly a whole bunch of people in the church started asking for my help. It... it was like all the church people had problems with their watches and clocks. I said sure, I'd be glad to help – and here's what is so wonderful – they said, 'take your time, just let me know when it's done.' They even paid me up front for the work, and they all said they're in no hurry! Now, how about that!" He pointed to a cuckoo clock on a nearby ironing board. "I've been working on that for over a year, but the folks at church aren't even upset with it."

He walked over and sat down on an old metal chair. "Yessir, I've got it good. I get up in the morning and work a little on my clocks and I play with my kittens. Then I work a bit on my watches and I go outside and enjoy the sunshine." He rocked back on his metal chair a bit, shaking his head at all of this. Then he turned to me and smiled. "Isn't God good?"

Yessir, Mr. Yates. And so are his children. Especially the ones at your church.

10.
California: Auctions, Falling, and Putting Your Foot in Your Mouth

Every day on the circuit was an adventure.

And when the adventure got underway, either I was a spectator or a participant.

Sometimes the adventures were awe-inspiring. Other times, they were, well, funny. As I said, I was either a participant or a spectator. In this case, I was a spectator – and glad of it.

Earlier in the day I had arrived in the Salisbury, Maryland area for a camp meeting, and the evening had been enjoyable in virtually every aspect. For one, the whole service was outdoors, with both the forest and night sky combining to make some very beautiful scenery. We were all under a rustic pavilion out in the country, listening to the crickets whenever there was a pause in the action. The college and career group, led by my brother-in-law Danny and my sister Gwen, had been wonderful. I received a great refreshing in my spirit when I sat with this group of around twenty-five rural young people who listened intently as my message centered on the service of a Biblical character named Epaphroditis. They humbled me with their intensity and seriousness, with many making decisions about entering into then-and-there service for the Lord at their workplace. Man, you cannot beat a feeling like when you see lives changed before your eyes. A follow-up call later in the year assured me that these young people meant what they said. They were servants.

But I can't stop the story there, or else I wouldn't be able to tell you about the activity that followed our meeting. We were going to have a bit of fun: an auction. The entire auction was indeed a treat, but an isolated incident *during* the auction was hilarious.

The leaders had gathered a small truckload of items and announced an auction. They decided on this event as a reward for a great year of ministry, and also just to do something incredibly nutty. Each young adult had earned points through various contests throughout the summer and now the points were turned into Auction Dollars, with each person getting around one hundred thousand "dollars." I was to be the auctioneer, and I took to this role with relish. I'm not gifted at this in any way, but I can speak fast, and so it fell on me to take the honors. It *is* a barrel of fun, building to something I can best describe as sort of like an organized riot, and I'd highly recommend it to any group.

"Okay, the first item we have here is a case of Utz potato chips, tasty to the lips but terror to the hips. Okay, let's start off the bidding at one hundred dollars..."

"One hundred dollars!"

"One hundred dollars to the gentleman with the polyester shirt he must've borrowed from his dad. Do I hear two hundred dollars?"

"Two hundred!"

"Two hundred dollars to the girl who fell asleep during my sermon."

"Two hundred and fifty!"

"Two seventy- five!"

During the opening rounds of the auction, I happened to notice an overly animated guy named Ralph who caught my attention for two reasons. One, he had to be over seven feet tall and skinny as a Number 2 pencil. Two, he had the loudest voice of anyone I'd encountered in over a year. Don't get me wrong - the boy wasn't obnoxious; he just had one setting on his volume and it was pegged to the level of F-15 Take-Off. Ralph would sit there and guffaw and brag about how he was going to win the case of Pepsi sitting on the table, one of the many gifts up for grabs. Hearing his chatter, I benevolently walked over and held I up so I could open it for bidding right away. He jumped to his feet in delight, but I heard a squeal from the front row.

"*No!* Don't put that up for bidding yet, Brad!" It was a twenty-year-old country girl named Phoebe who had recently been voted one of the group's leaders. She was clearly agitated about my starting the Pepsi bidding.

"What is it, Phoebe?"

"Don't do the Pepsi bidding now. Ralph'll just bid every thing he has and then leave. He's got to learn how to socialize with the group. He always leaves early." It sounded hilarious, but obviously she was intensely serious. She wanted to teach Ralph a lesson in manners.

Ralph hollered at a high pitch. "No, I *won't*, Phoebe! C'mon, let him start with the Pepsi!"

"*No!*"

"FEE-BEE!"

This was too funny, and I was going to play it to the hilt. I let Phoebe take the lead on this one. "Phoebe, whatever you say, since you *are* a leader. You don't want the Pepsi to be brought up yet, then I won't do it."

She nodded politely but her mouth was set in a straight line. "Thank you, sir. No, don't go to the Pepsi."

Ralph groaned audibly while everyone else snickered. I continued the bidding.

It was reaching a fever pitch. We auctioned off some Christian music tapes (remember, this was 1983), a Coleman camping lantern, concert tickets, suntan lotion, boxes of Hershey bars and some fountain pens. I reached for the Pepsi. "Phoebe, should I ..?"

She shook her head vigorously. "No."

"*FEE*-BEE!" came a wail from Ralph.

This went on for the next half an hour, to everyone's immense and sadistic delight. The little comedy continued through my auctioning off a radio, Yankee candles, Snyder pretzels, a Strong's Concordance, three stuffed animals, and a pass to King's Dominion amusement park.

I reached for the Pepsi. "Phoebe?"

"Phoebe, I *promise* I won't leave," Ralph begged. "Come on, now – the Pepsi case? Puh- *leeeeease?*""

Phoebe waved a dismissive hand. "Oh, all right, go ahead."

I no sooner held up the case of Pepsi when Ralph leaped to his feet.

"I'll give *one hundred thousand dollars!*" he screamed, his volume knocking over twin girls seated in the row in front of him. That was all he had; every point he earned that summer was going for that case of Pepsi. Nobody could match him.

"Going once... going twice...*sold*!" I roared. "It's yours, my man!" The group applauded politely.

He strode up to the front, cackled with glee and waved to everyone. "I'm out of here. I'll see you later, *chumps*!"

"I told you he'd do this," said Phoebe, waving him away. "Well, go on, then, country boy. *We're* gonna have fun."

The rest of the group nodded nonchalantly to him and went back to concentrating on the auction. There were plenty more things to bid on. I reached for the baseball tickets...

That's when I glanced out of the corner of my eye and noticed the change in Ralph's face. Something was wrong. He hadn't got the desired response he was shooting for.. He wanted people to beg him to stay... but he'd shot his wad. He *had* to leave, mainly because he said he would.

So he sauntered out slowly, trying to maintain his dignity. The rest of the group ignored him, chattering excitedly about the items left on the table. They were shouting, even chanting, for the bidding to resume. They had auction fever, brother. Danny and Gwen were in rare form, coaxing people to bid higher and higher, encouraging them with whoops and screams. The noise got louder and louder. In fact, the whole place was making quite a racket. The pavilion was near pandemonium now, with everyone yelling out their bids. "Let's get it going, then!" I shouted, and the crowd cheered. Things got rolling again. A calendar went for nine hundred "dollars." A golf outing went for seventeen thousand. A Baltimore Orioles baseball cap went for one thousand.

In the excitement of the auction, I forgot about ol' Ralph, but soon I saw in the darkness beyond the kerosene-lighted pavilion that there was a shadow lurking. When the auction got heated, the shadow moved nearer and knocked over an empty gas can.

"Who's there?" demanded Phoebe, who was fighting three people in order to win a bid of a kitchen wall clock that was Scooby Doo with rotating eyes.

Ralph stepped into the light, holding a fairly large cat. "I... er... found this tabby next to my motorcycle and didn't want to run it over..."

"Whatever," said Phoebe, turning her attention back to the clock in my hand. The kids all saw through Ralph's ruse; they didn't care either way. They went back to shouting and were now standing on their chairs. This burned Ralph even more. He edged to the back of the pavilion, holding the oversized cat who seemed totally disinterested in the social game going on, as long as it was getting petted.

Phoebe was fighting Maria for the Scooby kitchen clock. The bidding was up to thirty thousand... *forty thousand...*

"Stop being so cheap and make a big bid, Phoebes," called Ralph. Everyone ignored him. "Forty five thousand dollars," called Maria.

Phoebe was through messing around. Standing up, she shouted. "*Fifty thousand dollars!*"

I held the clock high. "Going once! Going twice! *SOLD TO PHOEBE!*"

A high-pitched "*YEEEEEEEEEHAAAAAW!*"pierced the air.

It wasn't Phoebe who screamed.

We heard the blood curdling war cry shriek come from the back of the pavilion, causing everyone to wince in pain. I didn't know anyone could scream that loud, but it was a doozy. Everyone swung their head around as they grimaced. It was

Ralph, with a mile-wide grin on his face. He got the attention he wanted; every eye was on him.

But that wasn't necessarily good.

In yelling his war whoop, Ralph forgot that he was holding a semi-feral cat in his arms. A cat that lived in the country with crickets, birds, and other quiet noises. It wasn't used to a fire-alarm blast right next to its ears. In the instant we swung our heads to see Ralph, the cat stood straight up in his arms, its fur standing erect, its eyes in a panic mode. This was not good for Ralph.

It unleashed its claws – we could see them from where we were positioned – and, so help me, went into a rotating round-the-clock motion with all four of its legs in order to get away from that ear-splitting noise. In doing so, it became a Living Buzzsaw. I had to admit, it was an awesome, if not brutal, sight. Our family has had quite a few pet cats in our day, and many of us got a slash now and again. But *this*. This was a sight to behold.

At the sound of that shriek, the cat became a flesh-ripping, razor-sharp instrument of pain in a moment.

For some reason unknown to any of us, the second it went into Killer mode, Ralph grabbed the cat and tried to keep hold of it. He may as well tried to bottle lightning. This cat was rotating, screaming, tearing and kicking – and all the time we could see Ralph gritting his teeth and clinging to certain destruction. After a full round of shredded shirt sleeves and bloody hands, Ralph let go. The cat miraculously flipped in mid-air and – you couldn't make this up – for a brief second they were facing each other eye to eye, about six inches apart. Like in the cartoons, both realized that they wanted to go in the opposite direction. The cat vaulted out of Ralph's arms while poor shredded Ralph turned to run, tripped his cowboy boots over one another and fell into the only mud puddle on the twenty-five acre property. Face first.

We laughed so hard, it took fifteen minutes to restore order. People were collapsing into fetal positions in comedic hysteria. And yet, though it was insanely funny, I had pity for poor Ralph in his situation, because both on the road and in my years of ministry, I'd also fallen flat on my face.

You know what I'm talking about. That little event or situation that puts you in a bad light. Makes you embarrassed. Leaves you looking foolish.

You remember? The time you came out of the restaurant bathroom with toilet paper stuck to your heel. Or when you sent a sensitive e-mail to the wrong person - or wrong boss . Or the joke you told where the entire party didn't understand it . . . or maybe misinterpreted it. *Badly* misinterpreted it.

OK, we're on the same page. You get where I'm coming from.

Well, one of those times happened back when I was in my first youth pastorate.

One of my kids fell out a three story window.

Let me back up. I'd better explain.

The year was 1981, and I had just graduated from Bible college, and my first ministry work was overseeing the youth in a small church in Hollister, California, then a quiet burg of about ten thousand people. One of my first tasks was to take the fifth- and sixth-grade kids to Bible camp in the northern part of the state. It didn't seem like too hard of a task, and I looked forward to spending time at the week-long retreat.

I remember the final miles of the trip to the camp.

"Hey, Pastor Brad, when we gonna get there?" yelled Shawn.

Shawn was my hyper kid. His usual school-time activity at recess was to run laps around the yard, just to wear off energy. Come to think of it, he ran laps in the classroom as well. Lots of energy, that boy. He was sitting there in the back seat of the van, chewing on a pencil.

"I've told you five times already, Shawn, we're almost there," I said, turning onto the exit ramp. "Calm down."

"He's telling Shawn to calm down," said Shelly. "Like that's ever gonna happen."

Shawn glared at her and started chewing on the back seat upholstery.

We arrived at the retreat center in our little church van, and the reaction was immediate: gasps of delight came from each of the middle-schoolers.

"Hey," said Ricky, "this isn't a camp. It's a giant hotel!"

Shawn gazed up. "Unbelievable."

Indeed it was. The retreat center stood at the edge of a lake. The middle of the center was a 1920s-era hotel, bought by the local Christian group decades ago when the hotel went bankrupt. It was massive. It was impressive. It had over 100 rooms and two towers. The main lobby had wicker chairs and a fireplace.

"Oh, man, the things we're gonna do," said Shawn, vaulting from the van.

I didn't like the sound of that. "Hey, wait, Shawn - " but he was gone.

"Welcome!" cried the head counselor with a grin that showed his back molars. "Okay, kids, grab your stuff and find a room down in the lower dormitory. Follow the direction signs. We'll meet right here in the lobby in two hours."

I stepped forward as the kids were being led away. "What happens in two hours?" I asked.

The head counselor winked and smiled hugely. "We'll let the kids have free time. Let 'em get to know the campsite."

"Um, I don't know," I protested weakly. "That means the kids don't have an activity for over three hours. Maybe I could take them on a hike or something right now."

"No, no," insisted the counselor soothingly. "We'll take care of all that. We don't want the kids to feel like they're burdened with too many rules. Now, you go and take a nice quiet walk. You deserve it."

My stroll took a half-hour, but I was uneasy about this. Thirty minutes without hearing from any of my kids made me a little suspicious. In fact, even fifteen minutes of non-contact made me real queasy. I glanced back and saw other kids milling about, staring at the lake and talking idly, but none of them were from my church. *Where were my kids?* I trotted up the brick walk toward the main entrance. I was getting nervous.

I glanced to my left and saw some kids who had discovered a soccer ball and were trying to get a game started. *Still not my kids. Where are they?* Then I looked to the right and saw Shawn walking toward me in a slow gait with a glazed-over look. Ricky came running up behind him, his expression frozen in shock.

"Shawn," I said. No response. "Shawn."

"*Shawn!*"

187

He stopped. "Shawn," I said, bending over. "What happened?"

"Um, well, we were playing hide and seek in the building..." said Shawn, still staring in the distance.

"Which they weren't supposed to do," yelled Shelly, walking over.

"And they trapped me at the end of a hall on the third story," said Shawn. "I didn't want to get caught, so I climbed outside of the window and hung on the windowsill by my fingertips."

"*What*?" I cried.

Ricky shook his head. "I couldn't find him in the room," he said, "but then I heard him yell."

I stood there, shaking my head. "W-what happened next?"

Shawn looked away. "I, uh, lost my grip."

We stood quiet for about 20 seconds.

"Shawn," I said, "you're telling me *you fell three stories?*"

"He landed on his back," yelled Shelly. "I saw it."

I was, as you can guess, stunned. "How come you're not hurt?" I asked slowly.

"Bushes," said Shawn, gulping. The realization of this was still creeping into him. "Lots of 'em, right below me. They broke my fall, just enough."

I went over and saw the thick bushes, completely with mashed foliage where his landing took place. He wandered around for a few more minutes, allowed me to take him to the nurse to be checked, and spent the rest of the afternoon on the front row of the chapel room, waiting for the speaker that night. Shawn wanted to make some serious decisions, and he didn't mind waiting five hours for the message to begin. A man doesn't go face-to-face with death and not come away changed.

As a matter of fact, he did indeed go forward and had some serious heart to heart vows with the Lord. I guess this situation ended up all right, but I was not only shocked at the fact that Shawn could have been seriously hurt, I was personally humiliated at the thought that I could've had a kid get injured – or even killed – on my very first outing of my ministerial career. Sort of makes you humble, you know?

My lessons weren't over, of course. I began getting new lessons in humility while on the circuit as I traveled, in many ways.

I had been back in South Dakota for a third time, and on this trip the local church realized I needed some rest, so along with a nice quiet home where I could huddle between my meetings, they gave me a pass to go to a health club at the outer edge of town. Boy, did I love that.

I had been speaking and visiting prisons and convalescent homes for about five days straight, but now I had a day's break coming to me. That morning I got up early, greeted the morning sun through the little trailer's window, and wolfed down a huge omelet, some toast, bacon, and two cups of coffee while I had my devotions. I was famished, but I was also ready to do some serious exercising.

I pulled on some gym clothes and jumped into the car. Within fifteen minutes I was running a circular track. After a five mile jog, I followed up with lap swimming in the club's pool.

Spoiler alert: Some of this story might be a bit indelicate so I'm going to apologize ahead of time. If you are of a stiff constitution, you'll get a good lesson from this anecdote, so please continue on. If not, move ahead to the next chapter.

It was still early as I wandered back into the locker room. I had finished a half an hour of vigorous swimming and followed up with some free-weight bench-pressing. *Aargh.* I plopped down and realized that I shouldn't have had such a big breakfast.

A middle-aged man wandered in and opened the door of a locker. "Morning," he said agreeably.

"Morning!" I answered cheerily although my stomach felt sour and I was trying to stifle a nuclear burp.

He looked at me for a few seconds. "Say, you're that guy who's over at Sunrise Church speaking this week, aren't you?"

"Yes, sir, I am," I said, hiccuping. I *really* wish I hadn't eaten that breakfast. "I'm surprised you would ... *urp...* recognize me."

"It's a small town," the man chuckled. "M wife went to hear you Tuesday night. I couldn't make it myself – overtime hours, you know." He bent over to untie his shoes. "So you're a minister? A parson, is that right?"

I heard him but I didn't answer right away. I could feel it coming from down below. My stomach was in kick-out mode. I darted for the bathroom stall and leaped inside, hovering expectantly over the toilet, my head leaning down and my legs trying to hold me up. "Well," I called over the top of the door, "I'm what you might call in a fancy term an evangelist, but..."

Oooooh, I felt bad.

"... I just like to say that I'm a guy who travels and shares the Bible."

I could hear him grunt that he understood. "So, can you tell me about the difference between a Baptist Church and a Catholic one?"

"Yeah, well," I called from inside the stall, steadying my legs and feeling the starchy acidic feeling rising in my throat and into the sides of my cheeks. I gulped but I knew what was coming. "For one thing, Baptist churches have pastors – shepherds of the flock, you might say. Priests are in the Catholic realm. With the Catholic church you have confessionals, and you don't with the Baptist, or Protestants..." I was woozy.

"Well, okay, that's what I had heard," the man said agreeably. I could hear him unzip the sports bag. "I've had some questions that I've always wanted to ask a man of the cloth."

And that's when I lost it. I mean, everything came roaring up the tunnel, brother. Niagara Falls was unleashed. Apollo 13 was launched.

To put it bluntly, I projectile vomited like I never had before. I believe I broke a bone in my ankle, I was shaking so hard.

"And what would you think would be a good way to go about selecting a church to attend?"

"I guess I would say that the first thing to consider is *BLEEEEEAAAAAAAGH...*"

So here I was, holding myself steady by clinging to both sides of the bathroom stall with legs that were shaking like Jello in an earthquake, vomiting in stupendous fashion while a man sat peacefully on the other side of the stall's door, happily putting on his flip-flops and asking me for Biblical answers on various questions he had been pondering for many a year. For reasons beyond me he never picked up on the fact that I was violently ill, nor did he seem to care that I was calling out answers from inside a bathroom stall. After ten minutes, he thanked me heartily and went out to the swimming pool.

That was one of my more, well, unusual counseling times. I learned that I could be put on the spot in any time and at any situation.

And I also learned how far into my mouth I can insert my foot. Boy, did I ever learn.

I was wrapping up a week of meeting in central California at a Christian school that seemed to have opened up to the Lord's prompting. The students were starting to respond, and I was happy to see the cold veneer of indifference break up. Flip, the youth pastor, had been having a hard time of it for over ten months, having the unenviable task of being both youth leader and school principal, neither of which he seemed to be able to handle well, nor did he seem to want to do anyway. To be sure, Flip gave it the old college try, but his heart wasn't in it, and in the ministry that can make a world of difference. The week was filled with his late preparations, little focus, and lack of deep interest in the task at hand. I could see why the kids had been getting cynical.

For example, one night was a gym night where Flip got the last-minute idea to serve banana and strawberry smoothies - from scratch.

And I mean *last minute*.

I was with him as he was throwing food in the supermarket cart with less than half an hour before he was to open the gym doors. He had no idea how to make these smoothies and was asking anybody in the store's aisles about it. He had no adult help in the kitchen. He knew there were over sixty kids coming to the gym event, but he made no effort to get any adult help, and I believe he thought that I would be able to handle the whole disciplinary affair. With a packed gymnasium and five playground balls, Flip calmly turned around, walked into the kitchen and shut the door while he and one other man - the bus driver - made smoothies from peeling bananas and hand-cranking every ingredient. They had not prepared any foodstuffs in the least, and it took forever to make them *one at a time*. The kids were slurping them down as fast as he could make them, and many of them never got any refreshments at all. The teens were in the gym tearing the place apart for almost an hour. I was running around, trying to referee the mayhem. I peeked in the kitchen to let him know I thought a teen girl was injured. He was leaning against a counter, stirring slowly and chatting happily, oblivious to the catastrophe going on in the gym.

It got worse as the week wore on. Wednesday night was the annual Graduation Banquet, a traditional wrap up of the year's events and memories. This banquet event had been a continuous school holiday for over ten years, the responsibility passed along to each new youth leader over time. It was a ties-and-tails affair with lots of pomp, and the teens all looked great on the night of the grand affair. Girls were in Cinderella gowns and guys wore fine tuxedo coats and even cummerbunds along with their ties or ascots. Parents came with flash cameras, and the senior pastor himself gave the opening greeting and prayer. This looked to be quite a fancy affair – until the program started.

Flip had waited until the last minute again.

Where do I begin? For one, there wasn't enough food. For another, the musical portion of the program - a string quartet - was given the wrong address and never showed up. The worst, though, was the main entertainment. As part of the evening festivities, Flip played a film instead of the usual trophies and speeches, as was the tradition. He wanted to show a movie instead. Not reviewing the movie, he showed sight unseen – I am not making this up – a 1912 silent film: *The Musketeers of Pig Alley*. (If you'd like to get an idea of how bad this movie is, I'd suggest you put down this book and find it on YouTube. They have posted the film in its entirety. I am sure you won't want to see the whole film.)

I am telling you that we sat and had to endure a silent film from the beginning of the history of film-making. Flip had misread the film's storyline.

It was grainy, jittery and had terrible overacting that resembled vaudeville-type emotions. I could see the adults looking at each other in the back of the room, silently wondering if this is what the kids nowadays enjoyed seeing for entertainment. The teens were dumbfounded at the theme of the movie and slid back into their seats, yawning. Flip gulped, realizing he should have checked this film. Kids ended up walking out of the room and wandering all over the conference center, bored out of their skulls.

But it's good to say that things got better as the week went on. Flip tightened the schedule and did a bit more preparation for each event. As I spoke throughout the week, I sensed a change coming over the student body/youth group. They were softening, seeming to latch onto the truth of the reality of the Lord and what He could do with their lives. There was quite a ways to go – for both Flip and the teens – but the beginning steps were evident. Some teens - even some adult leaders - made serious decisions and everyone was encouraged.

The week went by too fast, as it always seemed, but the results were happy to see. Terry was trying to be a better witness in his neighborhood. Kate wanted to join up with Sarah and read her Bible on a daily basis. Glenn was patching up a broken friendship with two other boys in the youth group, and Winnie had asked for accountability partners to help her stop gossiping so much. I had some sweet counseling sessions with a number of the youth, and I made some very nice friendships as well.

It was time for me to go. I was in my final message to them before I had to leave, and I wanted to make it extra special, with a real punch. It was a Friday morning chapel and I was full of energy and empowerment from the Lord – and maybe a bit too much enthusiasm. I was bringing home the points hard and true, and I had one closing illustration to use – a personal one that I felt would drive home the entire message.

I wanted to close with a final illustration with specific details so that the kids wouldn't feel I was being too generic.

I leaned forward on the pulpit. "Let me close with this charge to you, young people, about giving your individual selves over to God, because He'll bless the collective body of the youth group. Can I share a personal story with you? Last year I was a guest speaker for a youth meeting in a little town called Rampart, South Carolina. It was one of my most difficult meetings in any youth group I'd ever endured: the kids were stiff and uncaring, worldly and calloused. The whole place was a disorganized mess. The meeting started late and the room was filthy. I ended up having to discipline some of the teens because the youth pastor hadn't been doing it all year. In all, I openly questioned why there was a youth group there at all. It seemed like one big social event, and not one that truly sought God."

The teens were sitting there, open-eyed and especially attentive. *Good, I'm getting through.* I pushed harder.

"What a waste! Teens that could be growing in Christ instead fed each other's egos and formed cliques. They casually dismissed the whole message as if I were trying to sell them a toaster. Teens, you don't need to be like that youth group! Rampart had their problems and refused to deal with the obvious. You see the challenges before you – rise to them and seek the Lord for His guidance. "

The service concluded with some teens coming forward to talk with me. When they had gone back to their classrooms, Flip came over and nodded to me. "It's been a ... good week."

I smiled. "I'm encouraged. You have kids that are willing to make some changes."

"Yeah, that's true, true..." I could tell he was distracted. He picked at his teeth and looked up at me. "That was a pretty powerful illustration about that youth group in Rampart, where you spoke last year."

"Yes," I said as I packed my briefcase, "it really stuck with me."

"Did you...," he paused. "Did you realize that *I* was the youth pastor at that church in Rampart?"

My heart stopped. My ears pounded. I felt sweat popping out on my forehead as I looked up. "You couldn't have been. This was only last year."

Flip bobbed his head. "I've only been here a year. Less than that." He tilted his head. "I was the youth pastor of that group you talked about."

My head was swimming. It *couldn't* be. *What were the odds..?*

"Aw, Flip, there were scores of youth groups in that town, the chance that it was yours –"

"There was only one church in the area. If you remember, that was a tiny little town. I didn't get to meet you when you visited, but since you mentioned it during the message, I remember when you came and spoke. My pastor had arranged your speaking engagement. I was out of town that week." He shrugged.

I could feel myself blush deeply. "I am so sorry, I really don't know what else to say. If I had known, I never would have - "

He waved his hand. "No, no, don't worry about it. You were right, the kids *were* rotten. That's one of the reasons I had to leave."

My head was pounding. "Well, maybe the teens here didn't put the two together..."

He chuckled. "No, they all know I came out here from Rampart, South Carolina."

I shook my head, unable to say any more. I was too mortified for words. After mumbling my goodbyes, I shuffled out to the parking lot, got in and started the car. I had to make Illinois but I was at a quarter of a tank and had no money. And even if I hadn't made a vow to the Lord, I certainly wasn't going to go back say anything to Flip.

I reached up to adjust my mirror and found an envelope attached to it by Scotch tape. I opened it up and a roll of twenty dollar bills spilled out along with a note.

Brad –

> *Your messages hit home this week. Lots for us to contemplate. Lots for **me** to contemplate.*

> *Godspeed,*

> *Flip*

And I spent the next hour on the road pounding the steering wheel and my forehead. One of many lessons in humility I was to learn.

11.
Arizona: Joy of Speaking, Our Daily Bread and the Blind Pastor

I started learning to enjoy the small things in life.

A good, hot cup of coffee early in the morning.
A full tank of gas and a rain-free highway.
A nice, clean, safe, comfortable place to sleep at night... well, a safe place to sleep at night.

And a quiet time reading my Bible.

Since I did no television viewing beyond checking the weather at regional truck stops, I found that I was at a greater peace with my surroundings. It became evident to me that one of TV's chief intrusions into my life was in telling me who I wasn't and what I didn't have. That indeed was television's great battle with my mind and heart.

In fact, the circuit-riding ministry was a great mind-refreshing break of freedom from television. The lesson that I was learning was, contrary to what my generation was being told, that I didn't need to be dependent on TV. I used to watch the set and be told countless times an hour about the gadgets that I should be ashamed not to have ...but the fact was, I was getting along okay without them up till now, wasn't I? Yet I had a gnawing desire to get the latest and the best. I'd also see the actors and actresses strutting around in perfect physiques and picturesque lifestyles and be reminded that I was ugly both in appearance and in habit.

Then my circuit riding showed me how good life really was.

I was learning the power of the Koine Greek word *epiousios* that is found in what is known as the Lord's Prayer: *Give us this day our* **daily bread***.*

Epiousos is daily bread. I found that the phrase "daily bread" has two meanings:

a) the literal bread we need to eat to live

b) the figurative bread of those little energized boosts that help us make it to the end of the day

Simple, huh? Nothing otherworldly about this.

God *would* supply my physical needs. I *am* allowed to ask for the literal food I needed each day – and there indeed were days when I was woefully short on that. In other words, *I have permission to ask for little things.*

And in turn, *I can be thankful for the little things that God brought into my life.*

As an example, I thanked the Lord that I could speak.

I mean it when I say I was - and still am - thankful to be able to form words with my mouth. Please understand, I didn't thank the Lord for a dynamic ability to stir masses, because I certainly didn't - and still don't - have that ability. On the contrary, I thought that I was an average speaker even on my best days. In fact, I still hold that belief.

I meant my thankfulness for the power to be able to string sentences together normally. This hit home when I spent a Pennsylvania weekend with a youth leader who touched my soul. His name was Michael and he had a heart for teens like very few other youth pastors I'd met. Michael was energetic and creative. He was personal and dynamic.

But Michael stuttered. Stuttered *badly*. A birth defect had rendered his speech into a series of hmmmms and huuuuhs, drawing out even the simplest of sentences.

He faced years of heartbreak in trying to find work in local churches. Michael had been rejected by a number of assemblies for – in their words - his lack of proper discourse. Scores of pastors simply refused to believe a youth group would show respect for a stuttering leader. However, one church did, and the result was wonderful. Michael's heart for the teens was enormous, and I was amazed at his ministry. He and his wife Susan were in their forties, but their energy was amazing and their love for both the Lord and the teens was boundless. The youngsters returned their love, too.

The youth group was strong in the faith and solid in their commitment to his teaching despite the fact that Michael had a daily running battle with normal speech. His sentences were drawn out and even painful to hear sometimes. Where it would take me ten seconds to speak a sentence, it might take Michael a minute to repeat the same words. But I grew a great and grand friendship with this brother in the faith, and left Pennsylvania with the thankful heart of being able to talk without impediment. It also was a challenge for me – *look at how much Michael was doing despite his setback. Since I didn't have this handicap, couldn't I be doing more?*

I was also happy for the little joy of being invited to places.

I knew that these churches had no obligation to take on an unknown speaker who tooled around the countryside in a gaudy orange Dodge Aspen, but for some reason they did anyway. Even more so, while I was a guest at their locations, many church folks invited me to see the sights in their area. I got to see America through the eyes of the locals rather than a glassy-eyed tour guide. I got it from the *home folk*, brother. Through these many generous invitations I was honored to visit the Golden Gate Bridge, Mount Shasta, Yosemite National Park, the Badlands, and a strange places like the Corn Palace in Mitchell, South Dakota and the Westminster Mystery Mansion in San Jose, California.

I think I like best the places where I've been invited. I like being invited to people's homes. Not houses. *Homes.*

These church people knew I didn't have a family, so for one or two nights, they'd include me in theirs. In California, the Kliewers were a hoot to be around, always filling me with solid stick-to-the-rib meals and great stories. The Guerreros would invite me over for a no-nonsense Mexican dinner which still makes my mouth water in memory. *Quesadillas*, tacos, refried beans, *tostadas*. In Georgia, the Berry family sat me around the table and fed me apple pie and tales of their farming and raising seven kids. In South Carolina, the Wheelers gave me a key to their house so that during the week I could be in and out whenever I wished. The Cannons took me to see the Crazy Horse monument. The Daniels took me to see Mount Rushmore.

Then there was the older bachelor gentleman in Fresno who met me at the church and was straight up with me:

"Look, I'm gonna be housing you all this week, and you'll need to know right away that I can't cook a lick. So, instead, I'm gonna take you to a different international restaurant and get you some cosmopolitan background in eatin'."

And that he did. Monday it was a Greek restaurant where we discussed the Koine language while feeding on *halvas*, lamb, artichokes and thick coffee. On Tuesday it was Chinese eating, and the book of Revelation was the topic of discussion. Wednesday was Italian food and church evangelism. Thursday was French cuisine and prophecy. Friday was Mexican food and the miracles of Jesus.

Yes, it's a grand thing to be invited.

These folks – and many others – were displaying not only the spiritual gift of hospitality, they were showing one of the exciting attributes of God: *He's a God of Invitation.*

You'll see the truths found in both Isaiah 1:18 and Isaiah 55:1. And then we remember that Jesus Himself said "Come unto Me and I will give you rest?"

God invited Noah into the ark, where He was. Isn't that a great picture of salvation?

Best of all, look at Revelation 22:17. You know the main qualifications for coming to Him?

You must be thirsty and you must be willing.

That's it.

He's a God of Invitation.

After finishing meetings in Florida, I awoke at a truck stop in Pensacola and looked at my upcoming schedule. Opening my journal, I checked my next spot on the calendar and I saw that I needed to head back to the grand state of Arizona. I was scheduled for a week of meetings, and I noted that the church pastor wanted me to emphasize personal discipleship. I closed my calendar and pointed the car toward the west. I had a one-day chapel in Amarillo, Texas, and then a straight shot through New Mexico to Phoenix, Arizona.

As I pulled out, gassed up and checked the oil, I realized once again that my Aspen was running rough. More than once I'd had to refill the radiator, and the water pump was a concern for me. A few hoses needed to be replaced as well as a fan belt, but otherwise I thought it would hold up. Things were getting worse, though.

As I rode through Alabama, the wheel's alignment was bad enough to start the car shaking every time I hit fifty miles per hour. By the time I rode through Mississippi I was smelling odd odors coming through the dashboard. In Louisiana it was getting worse, and the car was shaking almost continually. The constant battling with the wheel and the smells were getting to me, and by late nightfall I pulled into a Louisiana diner and flopped against the counter, my head pounding. It was after midnight and the roadside eatery was nearly empty.

I propped my elbows on the linoleum counter and held my head in my hands as a friendly waitress came over. "What can I get you?" she smiled.

I lifted my head momentarily and squinted at her. My eyeballs felt like they were on fire. "Coffee, please. And something for a headache, if you have anything," I said while squinting.

Her smile faded. "All I can give you is aspirin."

I blinked against the glare of the light. "That's exactly what I'd like. Two, if you –"

I looked around. She was already gone.

Wow. She was already getting me the medicine. I'd tip her nicely, I thought. But she didn't come back. In about two minutes, another waitress came over and quietly poured my coffee.

"Say," I gulped against the pain. "Did the other waitress get my aspirin yet? My car's been running funny since I left a church back in Florida," I blinked, "and the constant noises and smells seem to have given me a headache."

The second waitress stepped back and blinked. "Oh."

I smiled weakly. "Could she get here soon? I need to make a church in Amarillo by morning time."

The second waitress was flustered. "Oh. She – uh – thought you were... well, the truth is, we don't carry aspirin, and she went back and –" She looked helpless.

Despite my headache I had to laugh. "No, please tell her I'm not drunk or fighting a hangover or anything."

The other waitress apologized profusely. I got my eggs and toast on the house, too.

The nice late night breakfast didn't do any wonders for the car, though. By dawn as I entered Texas the tires were fighting the steering mechanism and I was down to forty-five miles per hour on the highway. As I passed a farmhouse, I heard a shearing sound and the Aspen bumped heavily. I quickly moved over to the shoulder and got out. I groaned as I looked at a perfectly shredded tire.

I didn't even need to look in the trunk. I had no spare. I needed to call AAA Roadside service, but I was fighting time. I checked my watch. I had less than two hours until I was supposed to speak, and I was over forty miles away from Amarillo. There were no cell phones in those days, and I saw no highway call boxes. I was really, truly stuck.

Okay, Lord, what now?

Few cars were on the road this time of the morning, and the ones that passed me made it a point to look the other way.

In the old days I would have panicked or even become unduly angry. Instead, I shrugged and said a prayer. *Lord, I need Your help in a big way, that is, if you want me to make the chapel service in Amarillo.*

I looked down. I was greasy and rumpled from driving all night. I was tired and carrying the remains of a headache. I looked off to a side road and saw a farmhouse about a quarter of a mile down the lane. I started walking toward it.

I had no sooner come within twenty feet of the fence when I heard a growl and a snap. I looked down to see a medium-size dog of unknown breed latched onto my leg and pulling hard, whipping his head back and forth. I felt a bit of pain, but enough to know that he hadn't broken the skin. I hadn't entered a yard and was still on a public roadway. Was this a stray? Should I kick him away? *Are you allowed to kick dogs in Texas?*

"Rusty!" I heard a bellow come from the ranch house. The dog hesitated. "*Rusty!* Let him *go!*" The dog backed off and sat down, looking at me.

A portly man with glasses, salt-and-pepper hair and a cowboy hat stepped out onto the porch. "Sorry about that. He's over-protective. Are you hurt?"

I checked my leg. "Not really," I called. "Sir, can I use your phone? My car broke down and I need to call triple A and tow it into Amarillo."

He stepped off the porch. "Do you have business in Amarillo?"

"Yessir," I said, reaching into my coat pocket and pulling out a tri-fold brochure that told about my ministry. "I'm to speak over at the Avondale Christian School at 11 o'clock." I gave him the address and the phone number of the school. "Or at least I was supposed to."

He studied the brochure and looked at me as his wife came out on the porch. He handed the paper to her and looked me over. She adjusted her glasses and said nothing, reading every word on the brochure. She looked at him as he gestured to me. "Come on in, young man."

I stepped inside to a spacious home with oaken doors, wide hallways and the biggest sofa I'd ever seen. The floors were white tile and the kitchen opened up into the living room. Cathedral ceilings towered above me in the grand entrance. "Won't you come into the kitchen, now," said the wife, "and have something to eat."

"Oh, really, ma'am, thanks, but I'm in no shape – "

"Nonsense," she said, turning to the stove. "You go get your Sunday clothes from your car." She nodded to her left. "The bathroom's down the hall. Hurry now and get cleaned up. Breakfast will be ready for you."

I retrieved my clothes and took a hot shower in one of the most ornate bathrooms I can remember. Gold faucet handles on the shower. Embroidery on the hand towels. In no time I was cleaned and dressed. I stepped out and pulled on my tie. "I cannot thank you enough."

She nodded and put the last plate on the table. "Now, say your grace and have something to eat."

My eyes bulged. I was looking at a table loaded with eggs, bacon, cereal, muffins, jellies, pancakes and syrup. And a nice huge pitcher of coffee.

"This is, uh, quite a nice spread for the three of us. You're quite generous." I said.

"Oh, we already ate this morning," said the woman, who showed not an ounce of fat on her body. "This is for you, young man, so you sit down and eat up."

As I was enjoying the fine spread before me, the husband came back in. "I called triple A. Your car's already been towed to the garage right next to the school." I put the coffee cup down to thank him, but he pointed at the cup. "Finish that up, now, son, and get yourself over to the car in the garage. We gotta move if we're gonna make that chapel time."

The woman scooted me out the door with a pat on my shoulder and soon I was sitting in the front seat of a brand new Cadillac, jetting down the highway towards Amarillo. "It'll be close, but we'll make it," said the man, looking at the clock on the dashboard. "I called the school and said you were on the way."

He pulled me up to the front of the school building and nodded for me to go. "Hurry, son. You've only got about three minutes." I leaped out and then turned to thank him, but he had already pulled my door shut and was on his way. I stood there, amazed at the kindness I had been shown. A man had just traveled forty miles to take me to a school, after arranging for the care of my car. His wife had fed me the biggest breakfast I'd had in months.

And in all that time, I never got to find out his name.

Whoever you are, sir and ma'am, God bless you mightily.

I trotted up the steps and was met by the smiling (and relieved) principal, who immediately ushered me to the stage. I introduced myself to the student body and went right to the message. I had made it on time. As I stated earlier in this book, the Amarillo student response was powerful, with at least ten students making decisions for Christ. One of the girls confessed to me that she had been tangled up in drugs and was now fighting addiction; she wanted help. We were able to get her immediate assistance. Another girl, a junior who was one of the school leaders, admitted that she'd been playing the game of social spirituality. She had never made a full confession of Jesus Christ, and wanted to do so right away. A boy who was a senior wasn't sure that he'd ever made a decision to become a Christian. Before he left that office, he had made that eternal decision secure.

As I pulled on my coat and walked toward the front door, the principal thanked me profusely while also apologizing that he needed to run to the next class. He directed me to the service station next door, where my car was.

Okay, Lord. You've shown me why You wanted me at this school this morning. Would you also show me what I am to do next?

I entered the garage and continued to pray about what to do. I had no money for a spare. In fact, I had no gas money to travel much past the Texas state line. I approached the mechanic who winked at me and grinned a toothy smile. "Mister, you must have some good friends out there. The man who called in for the towing supplied a new tire on your car, and this here school paid for a spare."

Before I could utter any words, he turned. "They said to give you this envelope. They called it a fancy word, an honorarium, or something like that."

I was taken aback at the man's integrity. "Hey, thanks for taking care of that money for me."

"No problem at all," he said, still smiling. He breathed heavily. "Your Aspen will never make it to Phoenix. Heck, it won't even make it to Albuquerque. It's worked its little heart out for you, sir, but it's sinking slowly into the west, if you catch my drift."

I nodded. *Oh, I get it.* This is why he's been so kind. *Now, what kind of bill was he going to try to stick me with?*

He motioned for me towards the garage area, but surprisingly, he walked right past the Aspen, talking while he walked. "The school told me the work you do, traveling around and sharing the Bible. I like that kind of stuff, and I wanted you to know that I appreciate what you're doing." He turned and leaned against a pole. "You'll need a bigger engine if you're going to keep doing this riding around the country."

I raised my hand. "Well, now, look I –"

He gestured toward the other bay in the garage. "That's why I'm going to give you this car." I turned and looked at an army-green car that seemed to be twice as big as the Aspen. He popped the hood. "It's a 1975 Dodge Malibu Classic. It's older than the Aspen, but it's had twice the tender lovin' care your car would ever imagine. I've been working on it here and there for years and never knew what to do with it until I went and asked God what should be done. And He said to give it to you."

I looked at his uniform's pocket. It showed his name: Andy.

"Andy, I can't tell you how much this means to me."

Andy held up his hand. It had the title and registration in it. "Now you get on the road and get back to doin' what you're supposed to be doin'. I topped off the oil and filled the gas tank. Those new tires they donated? I put them on this Malibu. Oh, and the boys here, we threw an extra spare in the trunk. The way you've been movin' about, it looks like you need two."

Despite his gruffness, he allowed me to hug him. I shook hands with all the mechanics and headed out toward Phoenix in my second car, a Malibu Classic.

I arrived in Phoenix in the early evening, barely tired at all. My trip through New Mexico seemed like a lark. It's amazing what air conditioning and a radio can do for you. I was so happy to have a radio, I even listened to the Navajo nation broadcasts for over an hour, having no idea what they were saying.

I was now at Sunrise Bible Church, an established assembly that had a consistent ministry of many years. The assistant pastor met me as I entered the church offices.

"I wanted to meet you face-to-face and thank you for coming," said Gary Walker, shaking my hand. "I've been calling other churches around the country and they tell me the Lord's been using you in some powerful ways."

I chuckled. "Let's just say that we're all watching God doing His work. I'm just standing by the side."

Gary grinned. "Abraham's servant had the same attitude as when he found Rebekah and was telling of the miraculous journey. *'I being in the way, the LORD led me...'* Well, that's how God works best – when we stand back and let Him do the work."

"You got *that* right, brother," I said.

Gary walked me out of the church offices toward the building next door. "Brad, this is where you'll be staying this week. I was the one who arranged for your housing, and to be honest, a number of families wanted you to be a guest in their homes. I felt that you would get exhausted from having to cart your gear all around the city night after night, so I arrange for you to be right next door."

This eased up things considerably. Even though I loved to be in people's homes, Gary was right. Having one place – especially right beside the 'center of action' – would help me time-wise and even energy-wise.

"Wow," I said. "I'm impressed. You're giving me the parsonage to myself?"

"No, you'll be staying with someone," he said. "The senior pastor. He's my dad."

"Oh, I see," I replied. "How many are in the family?"

"He's alone," said Gary. "He's a widower."

Gary walked me down the driveway.

"And he sure could use a Christian brother about now. Here, let me help you load your stuff into the house and I'll tell you some more. He's out with some of the deacons on a hospital visit and won't be home for a few hours. I need you to know a little bit about my dad, Bill Walker."

After we loaded my gear into the parsonage, Gary motioned for me to sit down with him in the kitchen.

"My dad was the founding pastor of this church over twenty years ago. He was diligent and fatherly, and everybody in the community spoke highly of him. The Sunrise Bible Church reached into the community, especially in helping the homeless. Dad would organize meals and clothing for the poor. Mom was just as compassionate, and many times growing up, I remember her making two huge pots of soup – one for our family, and one for another family in town whose father lost a job or whose kids might have been in the hospital."

"Man, that's a heart of giving," I said. "Must've been a great home life."

Gary nodded and took a sip of coffee. "Oh, yes, it really was. That's the reason I'm in the ministry now – I wanted to experience the joy of what my dad and mom had every day. Working for Christ wasn't really work, you see, when you approached it like my parents did. Yes, we had a happy and active household.

Something new was happening every day. Sort of like your traveling experiences, I imagine."

"Absolutely."

Gary took another sip. "When I was sixteen my mom was diagnosed with cancer. Within a year she was gone. The whole church mourned; in fact, much of the local community did as well. My dad was heartbroken but I got to see a man lean upon God for the strength he needed in tragic times. It was a lesson I'll never forget."

"After three years," Gary continued, "my dad met a woman who lived across town, played a piano for another church. Her name was Barbara, and to tell you the truth, I think both church congregations worked hard to get the two of them together: church fellowships, conferences, picnics, stuff like that. It was funny seeing two churches try their hands at matchmaking. Well, it worked. Barb was an angel, I tell you. She had as much a heart for the Lord as my mom did. The next year they were married. I fully approved."

I sipped my coffee while Gary gathered his thoughts. There was something more to the story.

"They were married about five years, just as active here at Sunrise as any church couple could ever be, when the ministry began to gel in a new direction. Barb's special gift was in counseling. My dad was delighted to see this blossom, and he encouraged it at every step of the way. The ladies of the church took to her quickly, and soon Barb was spending much of her week in private sessions, helping women both in and outside of the church. She was a saint, I tell you."

He shifted the cup in his hands. "She had been counseling a woman who was not a member of the church. She had been working with her for about a month, a woman named Shelly. Shelly had been dealing with a number of issues in her life, and even professional counseling couldn't rid her of suicidal tendencies. Barb was able to make some breakthroughs, but she kept the phone by her constantly, because Shelly was still unpredictable in her behavior."

"It was early on an October morning when Barb answered the phone at home. Dad had just been called to an emergency hospital visit, and had taken the only car. Barb picked up the phone and found out it was Shelly. Shelly told Barb that she was carrying a gun and was going to use it on herself."

"Barb was able to get the location of where Shelly was, and it turned out she was only three blocks down at her own home. Barb sprinted down and ran the three blocks, bursting inside the house just in time to see Shelly turn around, gun at her forehead. Barb leaped forward to stop her, but Shelly turned to one side to avoid Barb's grasp. She twisted away and fired." Gary gulped. "Because of the angle she was at when she twisted away, the bullet travelled through Shelly's head and into Barb's. Both Shelly and Barb were dead immediately."

"I'm... I'm so sorry," was all I could say.

Gary bowed his head. "My dad was devastated. He preached the funeral, and it was at the graveside service that he realized that there was another tragedy coming his way."

"What could that be?" I asked.

"He couldn't read his notes." Gary looked up. "He had been to the doctor once and was told it was a possibility. It was a reality now. My dad was going blind."

"Trauma?" I asked.

"No, Brad, the doctor had diagnosed it months before. It was creeping into his eyes, but the doctors felt that medicines could alleviate it." He shook his head. "Medicines didn't, though. He's lost about sixty percent of his vision as of right now. It'll be gone within a year."

I looked down at the tablecloth. *Thankful for the little things. Thankful for being able to see.*

Gary pointed his cup toward me. "Brad, you're here for two reasons. First, we need you to bring God's evangelistic Word to us this week."

"Second, I need you to be a friend to a half-blind widower who needs someone to talk to. My dad spends so much time reaching out and serving others, he's had nobody to reach out to him. God's put you here for that purpose."

I can't recall a lot about the evening services in detail, but I do remember a pastor who would handle the Bible reading before I spoke, holding the Bible fully within an inch of his face while wearing glasses that resembled the bottom of Coke bottles. It would have looked almost comical if it weren't for the severity of his condition.

Each evening we sat and talked, for he couldn't watch television or even play chess. The first night he told me of his deep sadness of the losses of his wives. He talked about the fear of losing his sight forever. He shared how bittersweet it was to see the new generation come up and take the reins of the church: joyful because his son was one of those who were handling the responsibility well, but sad in that he was seeing his own body break down and unable to keep up with the many ministries he so dearly loved.

But on the second night he was quiet for the first hours we sat together. I felt that maybe he was embarrassed for sharing so much the previous night. After all, I wasn't even half his age; did he feel like he was sharing his heart with a kid?

Ten o'clock went by.

At ten-thirty he turned to me and asked:

"Now what do you think about the Redskins winning that Super Bowl? It was the seventeenth NFL Bowl championship, wasn't it? Man, they tore the Dolphins apart. That Riggins ran for 166 yards, did you know that?"

I laughed out loud. "Well, no, I thought he ran for 150 yards."

Pastor Walker waved his hand. "No, no, son, that was Franco Harris of the Steelers when he rushed against the Vikings. He racked up the MVP of that one, just like Riggins did at this one."

I leaned forward. "You know the NFL, do you?"

"Ask me any question," he said proudly.

"Okay, then," I sat back. "Who kicked the longest field goal in NFL history?"

"*Pfffft*. Like that's hard," he chuckled. "November 8, 1970, Tom Dempsey of New Orleans Saints kicked an NFL record 63-yard field goal against the Detroit Lions. It was at Tulane Stadium in New Orleans. His kick won the game for them by a 19-17 score."

While I sat there open-mouthed, he taunted me. "Come on, ask me something *hard*, boy."

And so it was for the rest of the week. If I couldn't stump him on football questions, I'd throw him something from baseball. Or politics. Or Italian food. Or Beethoven.

I came to find that what I thought would be a melancholy week of evenings actually turned out to be a series of late night Pringles-and-Coke sessions of useless trivia and hilarious anecdotes from his early years of ministry. We were whooping it up until the early hours of the morning every time.

I came into the office Friday, rubbing my eyes and stifling a yawn. Pastor Walker regaled me of his many malapropisms and blunders during such sacred events as weddings and funerals. I laughed until the wee hours of the morning.

Gary slapped me on the back as he saw me stumble a bit. "I'll bet you're glad this is the last night of meetings, brother. I know that between the preaching and counseling, you must be exhausted."

He put his hand on my shoulder. "And I really want to thank you for seeing after my father."

"I know it must have been terribly difficult."

12. Once Again in California: A New Way of Seeing, the Importance of Prayer, and the Boy Who Helped Bring Revival

The same came therefore to Philip, which was of Bethsaida of Galilee, and desired him, saying, Sir, we would see Jesus. - John 12:21

I sat at the rest stop outside of Phoenix, Arizona in the late evening hours, letting both the car and myself cool down before the overnight haul that would take both of us to Escondido, California. Sitting at a concrete picnic table and brushing away some loose crumbs from a previous family's meal, I took a few minutes to sip on a splendid cup of Maxwell House coffee and to do a little Bible study. Tonight I was exploring the passage in John chapter twelve, where verse twenty-one's message was especially striking, due to one small word: **see**. The Koine Greek word was *eido* and it carried a significant meaning for me as I was nearing the completion of my first year on my circuit.

Eido had four definitions that I discovered, and they could all apply to those who had asked Philip to see Jesus:

First definition: they wanted to become aware of Him with their eyes, to get a look at this Savior;

Second definition: they wanted to comprehend His power and goodness *by any of the senses*. Touch Him, hear Him, maybe even taste of a piece of bread or fish that He might miraculously make. In other words, they wanted to know Jesus in a way that goes beyond mere passing curiosity.

Third definition: they wanted to sense Him in their heart, take Him in their innermost spiritual being. They wanted to make this more than a vacation visit to a curiosity. They wanted this pilgrimage to help answer questions in their soul.

Fourth definition: They wanted to take a bold step; to discover Him, and with that discovery possibly find a whole new purpose in life.

I got excited when I read these definitions and began to realize the power of the Greek word *eido*. If I were to emulate those people in their *eido* pursuit of the Christ, it meant I would do more than more finely tune my eyes, mind, and attention to Him. I would also ascertain what must be done in my life once I'd reached the goal of this experience.

I closed my Bible and headed back to the car. The people coming to Phillip wanted more than a cursory glance at Jesus. They wanted an experience they would never forget. That's what I want, too. I'd been learning lessons along the way, and the support church-by-church had been nothing short of miraculous. Now it was time to dig deeper and discover new depths of understanding about this Lord.

The time was upon me. I would soon come to realize that I could have an *eido* experience of Jesus through watching a reflection of Him. It would happen in Escondido, California.

The excitement had already been building in the last forty-eight hours. I had been in my last day of meetings in Phoenix, Arizona, including a memorable day at a Mexican Christian school where I was able to enjoy a bilingual chapel and hear marvelous testimonies of students' great experiences in seeing

God's blessing. I was feeling that my cup was overflowing; how could things become more powerful than this?

Then at the host family's home, I received a phone call one early evening.

"Is this Brad Zockoll, the fellow who's traveling on a circuit riding ministry around the country?"

"Yes, it is. And who is this?"

"This is Dennis Sparks, and I'm the principal of Sinai Christian School in Escondido, California. I was able to look up your parent's home phone in Delaware and that's how I got your number in Phoenix. Listen, I need to ask you something very, very important."

I shifted the phone receiver to my other hand and took out a pen and paper. "Yes, Mr. Sparks, I'll do what I can. What is it that you need?"

"I need you to cancel your meetings in Seattle next week."

I held my pen in mid-air. "Sorry, sir, could you repeat that once more?"

"Yes. I found out that your next week's meetings would take you up into Seattle. I need you to cancel those meetings and head south, down the West Coast."

"Let me make sure I understand what you're asking. You want me to cancel the meetings I've already committed to, and come down your way. Is that correct?"

"Yes."

"Well, now, that's a pretty big decision for me to make."

"I'm sure it'll be okay. We've been praying about it down here and we're sure they're going to allow you to cancel."

"Why would you say that, Mr. Sparks?"

He paused for a moment. When he spoke, he pronounced the words slowly and with great gravity. *"Because, sir, there is a once-in-a-lifetime experience going on down in this Christian school. I've never seen it before. We're on the verge of a revival."*

"On the verge?"

"Yes. The Holy Spirit has been moving and it's evident in the hallways and the classrooms. You can see it in the students, from the seniors all the way down to the freshmen. The growing tension has encompassed the whole campus like a dam about to break. We feel that it will come through the words of a messenger from outside our campus and community. Through prayer we feel that person is you."

I let this sink in.

"This is indeed exciting," I said, "but as I said, the schools in Seattle will need to agree for me to cancel their engagements first. We scheduled those Washington meetings months ago."

"Sir, I want to tell you this in all sincerity. If you're wiling to come, then those schools will allow you to be with us. It just comes down to your willingness to travel to Escondido. The Lord will let those Seattle schools know that you should come."

I *was* willing. And amazingly enough, it was just like the school principal said. The Seattle area schools understood and agreed to cancel.

As I had mentioned earlier, that was when the excitement started building. I had seen some God-empowered events during my months on the road so far, many which came to my memory as I hung up the phone.

In Morristown, Tennessee, ten teens had made decisions for Christ.

At a Harrisburg, Pennsylvania Bible camp, nine campers made serious decisions for Jesus.

In Austin, Texas, eleven students turned their hearts to the Lord in salvation.

A West Virginia outdoor service saw ten parents get their hearts right and re-unite with their children.

In a Chattanooga, Tennessee camp, twenty-two youngsters came forward and gave their lives to Christ.

But I'd yet to experience a soul-gripping, all-encompassing revival that shook each and every person to their spiritual core. True revivals couldn't be manufactured – when they occurred, anyone and everyone would readily agree that it was totally of God above.

The way Dennis Sparks presented it on the phone, this sounded like something near to a revival. Well, we would soon see.

I pulled into the parking lot of the small building that housed the Sinai Christian School, an institution that held a little over one hundred in enrollment. I stepped out of my car at eleven o'clock on Monday morning, and the principal sprinted out the school door to greet me. Dennis Sparks was about twenty-five years old, with sandy hair and a strong jaw. He was of average height but he had an athletic build. True excitement was in his eyes.

He was pumping my hand up and down. "Brother Zockoll, Brother Zockoll, *Brother Zockoll!*"

I laughed at his excitement but raised a hand. "Please. Call me Brad."

"And please call me Dennis," he said, turning towards the front door. "Well, now. Are you ready?"

We entered the front lobby and I can honestly say that I could feel an aura of spiritual anticipation in the air. How can I adequately describe it? For those readers who have been in an actual revival, you'll understand when I say that I grope for the proper adjectives but can only come up woefully short. Although I put little stock on outward appearances and emotionalism, I could tell in the faces of the Sinai students that something important was in the works.

"Chapel time will be in about an hour," said the principal. "Please, follow me. There is an important thing I need to show you before you enter the auditorium to speak."

As he led me down the hall, I thought I'd try to get some more information.

"How did you know this was coming about?" I asked. "I guess a better question would be: *when* did you realize that revival was on its way?"

Dennis shrugged. "For the life of me, I couldn't tell you. I don't want to use a tired cliché, but I have no other choice when I say, it just happened. I can't truly give you a time or date, and not to sound high-minded, but I don't think anybody through Christian history could either, for that matter. I must say this, that although I can't tell you exactly when it was that the Holy Spirit was moving among the students this way, it was evident that something was going on." He stopped and thought for a moment. "Well, let me correct myself, now that I think about it," he said, leaning on a doorpost. "I can tell you something that gave a hint of what was to come."

"What's that?" I asked.

"Students started realizing their sin," he answered, holding open the door to a long hallway. "One by one I had guys and girls coming in private to talk about how their sin was grieving them. One fellow comes in and confesses that he'd been cheating on a test. A girl comes in to tell me how she wants to apologize to her teachers and her parents for horrid things she's been saying to them. A boy comes in and fully confesses, while asking for help from an addiction to pornography. Someone else comes in and makes a clean slate of dabbling with drugs. None of them had talked with each other; it was happening as if a great big cloud of conviction was hovering overhead." He nodded. "Yes. I would say we started to see the power of Christ move whenever sin was being confessed and forsaken – all over the campus."

We walked to a set of double doors. He knocked lightly and a thin boy of about fifteen years of age peeked his head out. "Yes, sir?" he asked quietly. In fact, I noticed that the whole school was unusually quiet.

Mr. Sparks motioned toward me. "He's here, Bennett. Our messenger is here."

The boy named Bennett stepped out into the hall and grabbed my hand with both of his. "Mr. Zockoll! It's *so* good to see you, sir. We've been praying for your safe journey."

I was taken aback at the genuine kindness of his remarks. "Thank you, Bennett."

"Please come on in," he said, pulling on my hand.

Mr. Sparks gave me a small wave. "I'm going to meet with the faculty. I'll see you later."

I stepped through the double doors and let out a small gasp. The room was actually a rectangular hallway of a sort, with no furniture. It was completely filled with students. Fifty or sixty of them.

All on their knees.

"We've been praying about the service today, and we'd be happy to have you join us in prayer," said Bennett. The room was so packed with students that I had to wait for some teens to adjust and shuffle around so that I could go to my knees and join them in prayer. Some guys and girls around me grasped my hand in welcome and a few patted my back.

A red headed fellow wearing a white shirt and blue tie motioned for the students to bow their heads. "Let's pray."

In the far corner there was a noise. I looked up. Was it a laugh?

The fifteen-year old Bennett jumped to his feet. I followed his gaze to the corner where two boys who looked to be about eighteen years of age looked up guiltily.

"You two," he pointed at them. "You need to get out of the room."

One of them raised his hands apologetically. "We're sorry, we really are."

"No," said Bennett firmly. "You need to go. Now."

I watched them get to their feet and pick their way through the crowded room. They both stood a foot over Bennett's height and outweighed him by a good thirty pounds each. They could

225

have torn him apart, but he stood firm as they passed him and went out the door. Nor did I see them show any rebellious attitude; they were submissive to his directive.

I looked up at him. "Wow," I said. "Pretty harsh."

Bennett's face softened as he got to his knees. "You need to understand, sir, how serious we are. We cannot have any compromise when we go to God to ask for His blessing today. We don't want any levity or lightness about prayer."

"I understand." And I did.

The prayers that went up were sweet and sincere. Students grouped in two and threes, begging God for His power to rain down in the service to come. They held hands and shared quiet but sincere prayers of faith, hope, trust and boldness. It was all about the power of Christ. It was a prayer of denying self and shutting down ritual or hypocrisy. The plea was for God to search each heart and show any sin so that the teens might recognize it and repent of it, asking for God's forgiveness and guidance.

I left the room stunned at the power of corporate prayer within those four walls. I had never experienced such a fervent time of prayer in my life.

And now it was chapel time.

The students filed in, and I'd like to say that the energy in the room was like the minutes leading up to the kickoff for the Super Bowl, but that's a terribly inadequate comparison. Few things in my life compared to the anticipation that electrified that chapel room.

The students sang a short opening song, after which the principal gave a short opening prayer in a simple but direct prayer: "Lord, take over the service. Take over. Direct in a way that will glorify You."

Dennis Sparks called me up to the pulpit. "And now our speaker for today."

I walked up with a deep sense of empowerment that was nevertheless blanketed by a monstrous feeling of inadequacy. Yet within these conflicting emotions came the spirit of sweet peace, held firm in the knowledge that none of this was about me. God was about to move through the service.

"I want to speak to you this morning about the holiness of the Lord," I said, "because of the many attributes of God, the one most often sidestepped by Christians is that of the Heavenly Father's holiness, but here we see it, in the Bible, page after page after page." I looked down and read the list.

"In Exodus 15:11 the writer asks 'Who is like You— majestic in holiness, awesome in glory, working wonders?'"

"In Psalm 47 verse 8 we read that God sits upon the throne of His holiness. In Psalm 60 verse 6 we see that He speaks in His holiness."

"In Habakkuk's first chapter, in verse 12 the writer asks 'Are You not from everlasting, O Lord, my God, my Holy One?'"

That was as far as I got.

As I looked up, I saw students moving out into the aisles and coming forward. Three, then seven, then twelve, then twenty... I stopped counting at forty. The Lord nudged me and I shut my mouth. I stepped back and was a witness to the moving of the

Holy Spirit through the lives of the young people. Children were praying deeply; some aloud, others quietly.

I guess it would be advantageous among many authors in Christian circles to insert their own actions and activities so that they might be able to put their personality in a strong light and even heroic light. I cannot even think of approaching that idea. When you have witnessed the power of God moving in people's hearts, souls, and minds, the one thing you realize is that you are merely a spectator. And that's what I was, one who stood back and watched the Heavenly movement among God's people. Teens were making decisions for salvation. Others were repairing relationships with fellow students and, yes, even teachers. The word "exciting" does not begin to describe the scene. It was serene and yet stunning. I was overjoyed and yet frightened.

The front of the chapel was blanketed with teachers and students alike, bowing in submission to a great and loving God, giving Him full reign in their lives.

These were the *eido* experiences I had been studying. But it wasn't over; that evening would complete the lesson that I was to learn when the Lord told me, "Be still, and know that I am God."

That evening was a time of all-church visitation, to be held at the Sinai Church, the overseers of the school's ministry. The church had started the school years back, and many of the Christian school's students were members of the Sinai congregation.

Church visitation has always been a challenging and rewarding night for me. This was when the members of the church would gather at the church and receive information from the leadership about people in the community whom those members could visit. Some visits were to be made at the hospital, seeing those with health issues. Others were for those unable to leave their homes, known as "shut-ins" whose visits would be homey neighborly visit with news of the church, a Bible passage shared and perhaps a basket of baked goods delivered. Still other visits were what might be termed "cold calls." These were visits to homes around the San Diego community in the form of invitations to the church or perhaps a more bold inquiry about the person's standing in the face of eternity. Cold calls were the most challenging, and the results are often unpredictable.

I was in the car with Dennis, on our way back to the church to join in on the church-wide visitation. Dennis was a member of the Sinai church and was an assistant to the youth program; in fact, he was in charge of the youth portion of the evening's visiting assignments. As Dennis drove to we spoke little.

"Do you mind if we stop by McDonalds for a quick bite?" Dennis finally asked, and I nodded. We'd easily run out of superlatives to describe the events of the day. Instead, we kept looking at each other and shaking our heads. It would be a day we would never forget.

"I'm looking forward to seeing the continuation of the revival when we get back to the church." I said finally.

"Oh? You mean more decisions?" He turned down a side street into a subdivision.

"No," I replied. "I mean the results of the scores of decisions that were made. You said there were almost fifty decisions this morning?"

"Yes," Dennis answered. "Fifty-six or fifty-seven, I was told."

"And most students attend Sinai Church?"

"Yes."

"Well," I said, "let's see how far their new commitment goes. Let's see if they follow through on their decisions by coming out to visitation tonight."

Dennis turned a corner and bobbed his head. "Good thought, good thought. Tonight the proof will be in the pudding, I guess, if that's the phrase." He pulled up to a small home and waved to a young man who was trotting toward the car. "I hope you don't mind, but we're going to have an extra guest coming with us to McDonald's and then to the church visitation. His name's Steve and he's fifteen years old. He's a student at the school –" Steve was pulling open the back door of the car. "– well, there's a story about him that I'll share with you later on."

We drove to McDonald's and this fellow Steve was a bundle of energy, sparkling and crackling and ready to get to the church. "Man, this is going to be a great time tonight, don't you think so, Brad?"

"Yes, I do, Steve, you never know what exciting things will happen when you let the Lord lead."

"Oh, yeah, good words, my man," he said enthusiastically while looking out the window. "Tonight will indeed be God in the driver's seat."

We pulled into the McDonald's and Dennis insisted on paying, so he handled the orders. Grateful, I set up the table with the napkins, condiments and whatever else you could set at a fast food booth.

Soon Dennis and Steven were sliding into the booth, doling out the evening's eats.

Dennis looked over at Steve. "Would you mind giving the prayer of blessing and thanks for our food, Steve?"

Steve's eyes lit up. "Oh, yeah, sure, Mr. Sparks." He looked down at the food, surveying it while keeping his eyes open and presenting his prayer:

"Hey, God, it's good to talk to You. We're over here at a McDonald's on – " he looked up for a nearby street sign – "West Valley Parkway, and we're having a little dinner before going out and doing ministry work for You. Mr. Sparks has a Big Mac, some fries and large Coke, and Brad here has a chicken sandwich – grilled, I think it is – and some fries and a Dr. Pepper. Me, I've got a Big Mac, some fries and a milkshake – it's a chocolate milkshake. Now, God, I know this isn't good food and some people would say it's junk, but I'm going to ask if You could bless it so that we can get the energy for tonight's ministry. And thanks that Mr. Sparks had the money for us to get this stuff. Love you, God, and I love Jesus." And with that he leaned over and started plowing into the food, shoveling fries into his mouth at an incredible speed. Dennis winked at me and motioned for me to wait.

"Say, uh, Steve, it looks like I'll need some extra ketchup. Would you do me a favor and go get me some, say about three packets?"

"Oh," said Steve, looking up. "Sure." He wiped his mouth on the back of his sleeve and headed toward the far side of the restaurant.

"I wanted you to see Steve up close and give you a quick background on this fellow." He leaned in toward me and cleared his throat before speaking.

"Steve had been a drug dealer for over a year on the streets of Escondido, moving narcotics of all kinds for his parents. They ran a crack house that was the center of drug activity in this area, but they never were caught by the police. Steve was one of the reasons. He was young, innocent-looking and smart as a whip, knowing when and where to hide. The kid was selling on the streets after school and on weekends, and I heard he was amazingly good at it."

"Last summer, one of our church members was walking around the block on visitation and happened to come across Steve standing on the street corner waiting to make another sale. Who knows how the conversation started, but God moved in like a lightning bolt whenever our man told Steve about freedom in Jesus Christ, the new life he could have, and the delivery from the bondage of sin."

Dennis looked me directly in the eyes. "Steve was bowled over by this message of Christ. He fell to his knees next to the man, called upon Jesus to save him and change him, and stood up with his hands raised in the air. He became a Christian."

"Steve was so excited about the life Jesus offered him that he took out his pocketfuls of drugs and threw them down the sewer grating. He ran back home and kicked open the door, shouting for his parents. 'Mom! Dad! Something happened!' he yelled. Remember, his parents ran a crack house and they immediately freaked out. 'What? What? Did you get caught by the cops? Were you robbed by another dealer?' they shouted. 'No!' he exclaimed as he ran into their kitchen. 'I just took Jesus in to my life and He's changed me! He's gonna take care of me! *In fact, He can take care of all of us! We don't need this crack house anymore! We don't need to do anymore selling! Jesus will take care of us!*'"

Dennis looked over at Steve, who was waiting in line to get the ketchup, and turned back to me. "They told me that his father was a big burly guy. 'That so?' his dad asked. 'Jesus gonna care of you?' 'Yeah! In fact, I threw away all of the drugs, threw 'em all down the sewer! We're free now! Jesus will take care of us!' Steve kept yelling. They say that when he told his dad that he threw the drugs away, the dad snapped. He beat Steven from one side of the house to the other, punching, kicking and slamming him. He shoved him through the garage door and smashed him to the floor and took every can of paint and oil and poured it all over Steve. Then he bodily threw him out the garage window – through the glass. 'Let's see Jesus take care of you now,' his dad yelled. "And if you ever come back here again, I'll kill you.'"

I sat back, shaking my head.

"Oh, wait," said Dennis. "There's more." I raised my eyebrows.

Dennis continued. "Steven picked himself up and checked his cuts and bruises, never complaining. 'Well, that Christian guy *did* say that Christians would suffer for the cause of Jesus, so I guess this is what happens.' Steve then made some amazing decisions. 'I need to get a job so I can get a place to stay. And I need to get an education about this Bible so I can understand more about what Jesus wants me to do.'"

Dennis tapped the table with his finger. "Brad, Steven refused any charity, feeling that's not what a disciple of Christ should do. He met with an older couple and worked out a living arrangements and their overseeing of him. Get this - this young man went out and got himself a job in the evenings so that he could rent a room in their remade garage for his 'apartment,' and he took on extra work so he could pay for his tuition at Sinai."

"Wait," I said. "You mean, he's paying for his own schooling – and he's not even sixteen?"

Dennis nodded as he saw Steven coming back. "Yep. He gives the money to the elderly couple each month. He's paid up to date." He tapped the table with his knuckle. "I believe Steven is one of the key reasons revival has come to our school."

After our meal we headed to the church. As we entered the auditorium I smiled. The effects of the revival were beyond emotion. There were more than forty students standing in the auditorium, ready for visitation.

After a joyful prayer the senior pastor handed out the assignments for the night. Adults played the part of chaperone and visitation leader for each car. All vehicles were stuffed with enthusiastic teens ready to do God's work and see His power in action.

My Malibu was also packed shoulder-to-shoulder with kids. Steve was in my car as well, thanks to Dennis. I looked at the map and got in line with the caravan of vehicles. Our assignment was in a subdivision in San Diego that had not been approached by the church in years. We were heading into virgin territory, as they say and Steven could hardly wait.

The traffic wasn't bad, and the weather was great, but as we navigated the streets I could hear Steve mumbling, "Let's go, let's go, *let's get there.*" I didn't find it disrespectful at all; in fact, I was humbled by the respect and submission that Steve showed to me throughout the evening up to that point. He wanted to be taught in everything in the Bible, and he looked to any authority to help him in his quest.

We found the subdivision, and that's where the action started.

I had not even brought the car to a full stop when Steve burst open his door and sprinted to the first house on our route. I mean, he *sprinted* – took off and dashed towards the nearest house, leaving my car door still open.

As the other teens piled out and I went around the car to close the door, I looked up and saw Steve vault onto the porch of the nearby house. With both fists he impatiently pounded on the screen door. A forty-something pudgy man in a T-shirt opened the door, eyebrows raised.

"I need to ask you something, sir," said Steve, with an urgency in his voice. He pointed at the man's face. "When you die, are you going to Heaven or Hell?"

The man paused for a second and looked up at the clouds. "Well, now, that's an interesting question that really has no answer." He closed his eyelids halfway. "You know, there are many different routes to take to answer that –"

Steve threw up his hands in disgust. "*Aaaaaahh!*" he groaned, frowning as he turned off the porch and vaulted over the man's flower bed, running to the next house.

The man stood speechless. I can't say I blame him, either. How else would you respond if, on a quiet evening, you were startled by a wide-eyed who teenager pounded at your door, pointed in your face and demanded to know about eternity? How else would you act if that same teen leaped off the porch and ran away before you could get a full answer out of your mouth?

"I'm so sorry, sir," I said as I scooted up to the porch with another teen. "We're from Sinai Church down the road, and that fellow's a bit overenthusiastic. Here's Tanner – he'll tell you a little bit about us." I pushed Tanner towards the puzzled man as I leaped off the porch in pursuit of Steve.

He was already at the second house, pounding away on the screen door. As I scrambled up the steps, he was met by a lady who was holding a dish towel in her hand. He gave the same introduction: "I have one question to ask you. When you die, do you know if you're going to go to Heaven or Hell?"

She rubbed her hands on the towel and squinted. "Well, I look at it this way. Nobody can really know these things. I call myself a relativist, and I feel that the afterlife is mostly guesswork –"

Steve again threw up his hands in disgust. "*Aaaaahh!*" he yelled, turning and vaulting off of the porch. She stood frozen, trying to comprehend what had just happened. I slipped in quickly with a deep apology and produced another teen to introduce the church in a more civil manner.

This time I caught up with him as he was leaping onto the porch of the third house. "Steve, Steve," I gasped as I grabbed his shirt and pulled him back. "You can't approach people this way."

He stopped and looked at me blankly. "Why not?"

"Because," I said, catching my breath, "there's a more gentle way to introduce the Gospel to people."

He shook his head. "They're playing around, man. If they're not gonna get serious about eternity, I don't want to waste my time with them."

"People need to be reasoned with," I said. "They need explanations, and often that takes time. You need to hear them out and gently take them through the Scriptures."

"Ah, there's so much to do, man, there's *so* much to do." Agitated, Steve ran his hands through his hair and squeezed his eyes. He took a breath, looked me in the eye and waved his arms toward the row of houses.

"Look, Brad, look way down here. Look at how many houses there are out there? How many do you think?"

"Hundreds, Steve," I said. "No, thousands."

Steve nodded, gulping. "We have *so* much work to do." He looked down the street. "So much work. And I don't have time to mess around with people who aren't serious about their eternity. I want to reach people who *need* to know, who are *looking* for the Answer." He looked back at me. "Doesn't that make sense?"

And I slowly nodded my head.

Yes, Steve, it made sense. Steven, *you* make sense in this crazy world of churches that are obsessed with numbers and programs and music-fests and brightly-lit stages and leaders who adopt an odd wardrobe and a puzzling lingo. Unknowingly, Steve, you became my teen version of a John the Baptist image, flying in the face of ecclesiastical politics and one-upsmanship and pharisaical desires for glory. I mulled all night over this boy's urgency to get out the Word. It sank deep into my gut and gave me new insight. I was experiencing *eido* through one of Jesus' children.

Steve, you'll never know how much you made a breakthrough for me.

You showed me a heart intensely devoted to Jesus, and Jesus alone. Your fervent desire for the Lord was a soul-gripping lesson for me on the road, opening up my heart to see the real reason we all do this work.

It was defining moment in my life, brought to me by a fifteen-year-old boy.

Steve helped me see the pure, exciting, fervent work of the Kingdom once again.

Once again, the week was too soon over. The many other amazing things occurring that week will be reserved for me to tell at another time.

Now it was over, and I sat in my old but trusty Malibu, turning over the thoughts of the most dynamic week I had experienced on the road.

Then I looked through my wallet. I had no money, and I needed to get to Michigan. The school had no money to give me.

Well, Lord, I guess I'll see what You'll do now.

I pulled my car to the edge of the gravel parking lot, my headlights pointed towards Detroit, Michigan. Looking right and left to see that the highway was clear, I paused for a moment when a flicker of activity in the rear view mirror caught my attention. I adjusted the mirror and saw a dust cloud coming toward me. No, it was a person running, raising the dust. Running with all his might.

It was Steve.

I put the car in park and rolled down the window.

He scooted up to the window and leaned in. "Brad, I can't tell you what it meant for you to come and be a part of this week. We've all seen God work and we'll never be the same."

"Steve," I said with emotion. "You'll never know what your enthusiasm and Godly determination have meant to me. I will carry the memory of my time with you to the day I die."

He thrust his hand in the window and shook my hand. When I pulled it away, I found my palm filled with ten dollar bills.

"No, Steve, I can't take this money."

"You *gotta*, Brad."

"No, I don't, and I *won't*." I paused. "I... I *know* how hard you're working and how you're spending your money on tuition and-"

Steve set his jaw. "Brad, God told me to give you that money, and I'm giving it to you. Are you going to go against God?"

No, I wasn't.

I pulled out of that parking lot, waving my hand out the window and watching Steve in the rearview mirror, standing there grinning and returning my wave.

I cried for the next hour.

But I was also smiling.

13.
Tennessee: Asleep at the Wheel
and the King of the Hill

I was travelling to Orangeburg, South Carolina and had been racing to make it to the morning meeting. I was due to speak in South Carolina for the next three days and my first engagement was to speak to a school group within six hours. The problem was, I was still *five* hours away, according to my map. I once again realized a huge error I had made in my enthusiasm to book meetings. I had said "yes" to yet another request, not taking into consideration just how large the United States actually is. Or how tired I could actually get.

My last meeting had been in Nebraska. I had been driving nonstop all day and night to make it to South Carolina. Or was it two days? The only sleep I had grabbed – when I realized how close I would be cutting it – was a one-hour snooze in a rest stop along Interstate 95. It wasn't great.

So here I was, racing along the highway, pushing the car and my body to make it in time to speak in Orangeburg, South Carolina.

As the morning dawn brought a soft light ahead of me, I glanced up the road and looked to my right at something that caught my attention.

The forest. It was moving.

The trees were standing up taller, breaking away from the group and moving. Marching, really.

I gripped the steering wheel tightly. I was watching pine trees getting up and marching toward the highway up ahead of me. *I had never seen this before.* As I drove in that direction, I was transfixed. *What would they do next?* I got my answer in stunning reality when I saw the gigantic marching pine trees *open their mouths and start to chew and swallow the road only ten miles ahead of me.*

I was now perplexed. *How would I get to Orangeburg if the pine trees had chewed away my side of the highway?* They seemed to be doing a good job of it.

I stared in disbelief and even in anger until my sleep-deprived mind realized that I was hallucinating in broad daylight. I swung into the next rest stop and made the phone call to Orangeburg.

To my chagrin, I had to admit that I could not make it that morning. Perhaps we could delay the meeting a few hours? The church was quite accommodating.

I found out through the months that there were other churches – and police – who were extraordinarily polite considering the fact that I was falling asleep at the wheel. In one instance, a pair of California policemen stopped me and searched my vehicle while I explained that I had finished a meeting in Oakland (it was three in the morning and I was over four hundred miles away) and was heading down the coast. I was still in my suit and tie, but I knew full well that this only made me appear to be a travelling businessman who may have had a few too many drinks at a local tavern before hitting the road. This idea, at the time, seemed funny because I've never – even before I became a Christian – touched a drop of booze in my life. The policemen were firm and curt until their flashlight beams fell on the Bible and notes that I had sitting in the passenger side seat. For reasons unknown to me, they fell all over themselves apologizing. With polite nods they encouraged me strongly to find a nearby coffee shop and get some caffeine in me.

My unbreakable schedule was wearing me out. With no organization offering me finances or setting a pace to my speaking schedule, I had no governor on the race car; I couldn't figure out how to slow down. I was pushing it too hard and the fatigue was soon catching up with me. I fell asleep at a table lunch with some folks in Oakland, California and had to excuse myself.

Once, while staying with a host family in Georgia after a series of meetings in the Gainesville area, I overslept and nearly missed a meeting because a grandmotherly woman snuck into my bedroom and shut off my alarm clock – the one I had set for 4 a.m. – because she figured I would need the sleep. I awoke an hour late with one hundred miles to go, dashed through a shower and pulled on my clothes, screeching out of the driveway and zooming through the many subdivisions that surround Atlanta. When I made it to the Interstate, I realized I was still half asleep due to the fact that I whipped into a truck stop to get gas but didn't end up at the pumps. Instead, I took a wrong turn and found myself parked neatly on the front lawn of their property. I got a few stares.

I was pushing hard, but I didn't know how to pull the reins. In one of the only times I rented a hotel (the one I mentioned in Centennial, Colorado, and it was due to increasing fatigue), I was on the phone with my mom, giving her an update, when a black medium-size dog – a collie, I think – ran from the front of the hotel door past me and into the bathroom. As my mother talked on, I blinked. *Had a dog just darted through a locked door and sprinted into the bathroom, or was I hallucinating?*

"Mom," I said as calmly as I could. "I'm going to go check the bathroom to see if a large black dog has darted into my room. If so, I've got to wrestle him out of the room. If it's not a dog, I've just seen one of the most vivid hallucinations I've ever experienced and I've got to get to bed. Either way, I think I'd better hang up."

I hung up. I checked.

He wasn't there.

I went to bed.

I was forcing myself to slow down a bit, but the adventures never stopped. Neither did the lessons.

One of the great things about circuit-riding to small churches was that I'd often get the opportunity to do so much more than just speak. Many times there would be an additional activity coupled with my visit such as a church anniversary, a youth rally or a homecoming (a celebration quite popular in Southern congregations), and it allowed me to roll up my sleeves and contribute in ways other than behind the pulpit. Assistant chef, builder of VBS backdrops, lawn-mowing team member, game referee, talent show emcee, junior carpenter, amateur painter ... I was building quite an impressive blue-collar resume.

When I arrived in Cookeville, Tennessee, I happened upon one of these opportunities. When George, the youth leader, gave me the low-down, I clapped my hands with glee. The special event on Saturday was a special multi-church youth rally called Slop Day, a standard among many youth pastors of the late 70s. The idea was to have all of the activities centered around mud; volleyball, tug of war, football, relay races were all staged in a mud pit or muddy field. Teen participants and adult referees alike would end the day with a muddy sheen from head to foot. Every Slop Day I attended was enormously grimy and delightfully grubby, and the Cookeville meeting looked to be just as outrageous.

Four churches were attending the events, with an estimated attendance of about one hundred and twenty teens. George had an apologetic look.

"I know you're speaking during the early Slop Day activities, but this event grew bigger than I thought, and it's putting a strain on me. I've come to ask you for help beyond your speaking time. Uh... we're a bit shorthanded and I wanted to know if you'd like to be one of the referees."

I leaped at the chance. "Definitely, George, definitely!" I sounded like a junior higher being asked about tickets to Disney World. I was embarrassed that I gushed so openly, but then again, hey – this was *Slop Day*, brother.

On Friday afternoon as I viewed the adults hauling hoses and spraying water on the playing areas containing a mud pit, water/mud slide, and mounds of sludge, I knew it was going to be a day to remember. I also knew that *I* was guaranteed to be spattered with muck and slime, but these events were always hilarious, and being a referee gave me a front row seat to the action.

Saturday arrived.

"Here you go," said George, handing me a referee shirt and whistle. "You'll be speaking early in the day, before the games get started, obviously. Then you've got the King of the Hill duties."

He pointed to that gorgeous mound of muck. "Right now, though, we've got to get all church groups familiar with what'll be going on. Could you help acquaint the various church youth leaders with the ground rules – no pun intended – for the day?"

As the numerous church buses pulled up and the Cookeville church's youth staff handed out programs of the day's events, I straightened my clean striped referee's shirt and strolled over to each youth group leader, welcoming him and helping to explaining the rules for each game. Tug of War was a pretty simple explanation, as was the mud slide. It was when I got to the King of the Hill game that I saw a fussing in the group to my left. I looked over, puzzled, and immediately recognized some old friends.

I knew Lou Felts and his wife Sally from a previous series of meetings I had in Tennessee. I happily waved to them but my greeting was not returned. These youth leaders were preoccupied and agitated about something.

"Hey, guys. Is there a problem?" I approached Lou and Sally and gestured toward the giant mound. "The game's a pretty simple one. You see that twenty- foot high pile of mud? That's the one where I'll be head referee. At the whistle, the guys all scramble for the top, and pull, push and grab to keep that spot up there. After two minutes I blow the whistle. Whoever remains at that peak is the winner." I shrugged. "That's it."

"Yes, and that's my problem," blurted Sally.

"What could be the problem?" I asked. "The boys are all wearing old clothes. We're only taking volunteers of teens who want to get involved. Nobody's being forced to play. Look, Sally, all the boys who have signed up are sixteen and seventeen years of age."

"Like I said, that's my problem," she fumed. "Rather, *he's* the problem." She jabbed a thumb at her husband. "He *insists* on playing that King of the Hill game."

Lou shook his head and grinned goofily. "Yep. I'm going to."

I took a look at Lou, who I'd known for almost two years. He was a likeable guy who came to Tennessee from Indiana, and he'd been working with youth people all his life. And that was a pretty long time. Lou was over forty years of age, slightly balding, with a nice coffee-and-doughnut-enhanced paunch. I knew Lou well enough to know that he hadn't had any daily exercise beyond going to the church refrigerator every 45 minutes for a bottle of water.

And a handful of nursery animal crackers.

And a slice of leftover cake from the Senior Saints' "Happy for Autumn" party.

I raised my hands and lowered my voice. "Now, Lou," I said carefully, "you don't want to do this, man. Some of these boys are varsity high school football players. The prize is substantial and these guys aim to win."

He chuckled and waggled his head, shaking his small but noticeable double chin. He pointed at the huge grimy mound. "Put me at the peak of that mountain to start the game," he said, "and just watch me."

"But Lou, listen to me," I protested. "We've got some beef-fed young bucks snortin' and ready to roar. They want to show off in front of the girls, and that's always a factor that'll include possible violence. These boys aren't going to do you any favors. And that's twenty feet of mud, buddy."

"Put me at the *top*," he repeated, more sternly. "And just *watch* what I can *do*."

I looked helplessly at his wife. She shrugged and threw up her hands. "If he gets hurt, that's his problem," she said, wandering off to the snack table. "I just don't want to hear any whining afterwards,' she yelled over her shoulder.

The afternoon's activities went without a hitch. The mud pit was four feet deep and over seven feet long, so the Tug of War was a blast. Whole teams went into the trench, floundering and sloshing and making a good old mess. We had a pie-eating contest and a water balloon fight that added to the sludge. In fact, by the time the mud slide competition was complete, virtually everybody enjoyed the unique ooze-covered camaraderie found in getting downright filthy through every layer – and I mean *every* layer – of clothes. I looked down and saw that my referee's shirt was a spattered mess and my shoes were caked. I was digging globs of grit out of my hair. Hey, things were looking good. Good thing they had me give the Bible message earlier – nobody would be able to enter any building unless they got completely hosed down. I checked with our staff. No injuries. No fights.

Now it was time for King of the Hill.

The crowd gathered around the large pyramid of muck and started chanting, ready to watch the fun.

"King of the Hill."

"King of the Hill."

"King of the Hill."

A dozen teenage guys, limbering and stretching, ringed the base of this little mountain.

I was hoping that Lou would forget his idea of participating. Or at least be counseling a kid so he wouldn't make it in time. Glancing about furtively, I was relieved when I couldn't see him anywhere. Emboldened, I blew a short *tweet* on the whistle and called the group of participants to gather in front of me.

"The rule to this game," I announced over the increasingly loud chanting, "is to be the one who is at the peak at the end of two minutes. You'll know it's over whenever I blow three long blasts on the whistle. Okay, guys, the limits are kind of obvious. No biting or scratching. No gouging. Pulling and tackling is okay, but punching and temper tantrums are out. Everybody ready?"

The guys nodded their heads and grinned in a way that made me shiver. "Okay, you can go get your place anywhere along the base," I said, "and start up the hill at the sound of the whistle." I glanced at the top. *This would be fun to watch.*

But when I looked up at the peak, I groaned inwardly.

There sat Lou, wearing a too-tight T-shirt and that goofy grin. He was sitting firmly at the peak of the mountain with his boots dug firmly in the wet mud. The teen spectators smelled blood and were chanting insanely.

"*King of the Hill! King of the Hill! King of the Hill!*"

"Lou..." I shouted in protest.

"Ready to roll, man," he called to me.

"Get yourself killed, then," shouted someone from the thick of the crowd. It was Sally, glaring and eating a hotdog at the same time. It was an unattractive combination, because she was chewing in anger.

I looked around at the boys. They were viewing Lou with a look that a lion gives to a wildebeest with a gimpy walk. I viewed the faces in the crowd. The mud-spattered faces were eager with anticipation.

I blew the whistle.

Encouraged by the maniacal screaming, the teen boys scrambled and slipped up the muddy slope. They soon were flopping and sliding to the bottom, thanks to the fact that three workers wet the mound again with water hoses for a good half hour before the game started. Clawing and digging their way up the mountain, the boys heaved themselves toward the pinnacle.

And Lou.

The crowd was screaming and jumping.

Lou sat there like a fat Buddha waiting for his adherents. As the first boy got within reach of the summit, Lou simply leaned forward and shoved the top of the boy's head. Without anything to grab, the fellow slid back about seven feet. Another lanky kid came within arm's reach, but again, Lou popped the crown of his head with the flat of his palm, and the kid slid backwards halfway down the hill. He looked at me and winked. The kids cheered lustily. Lou had this game figured out.

Two boys, whom I'd recognized as twins named John and Jimmy, approached the top simultaneously, and Lou met them with head-shoves that sent them both tumbling and sliding to the very bottom. They splashed in the goo for a moment before gathering themselves together for a huddle. I kept an eye on them, watching as they gestured to each other as boys were sent spinning down the slope nearby. After a few more words and a nod, Jimmy sprinted to the back of the mountain while John clambered up the front, shouting and pointing at Lou.

"You're mine, old man!" shouted John, grinning wickedly. "I'm getting you this time!"

Lou saw him coming and grinned. "Bring it on, little boy. I'll send you down again!"

Another easy kill, thought Lou.

But John was a decoy.

While he scrambled up and made a feint at attacking Lou, Jimmy had slithered up the back of the mountain unnoticed. Just as John came within reach of Lou's waiting strike, he rolled quickly to the right. Lou had completely fallen for the ruse.

The next part of the story I will relay to you in slow motion for better detail. *Excruciating* detail.

For a moment – as in virtually every person's memory – there are certain incidents that teeter on the fine line between career-ending disaster or a beautifully hilarious story to be retold by firesides for decades to come.

This was a fireside story.

From behind, in a superhuman effort, Jimmy leaped up in the air *over the top* of Lou's head – I am not making this up – and fell into his lap, headfirst. He clutched whatever he could, which was Lou's legs. Specifically, he clamped his arms behind Lou's knees and clutched them to his chest.

For whatever reason, in a split second of time, Lou in his confusion did exactly the same thing. As he saw Jimmy's legs in front of his face, he grabbed them and pulled them toward *his* chest.

This made for an interesting picture, if you can visualize it: Two bodies are facing each other with one's head clamped against the other's knees and visa versa. Gravity is coming into play at the top of a wet muddy hill. The two bodies are teetering due to the inertia of Jimmy's leap.

So help me, Jimmy was fully upside down. And Lou was falling forward.

Have you ever seen a Slinky bounding its way down the steps of your home?

Okay, you're getting the picture. Jimmy and Lou flipped end-over-end down the twenty-foot mountain, whacking the side of the hill with each flip. Flip *whack*. Flip *whack*. Flip *whack*.

That in itself could have made a good story. But the truth of the whole incident was that Jimmy was able to safely tuck his face hard against his own shoulder, saving himself from the shock of each Slinky-smack all the way down.

Lou, however, had not reacted so fast, and his face was pressed loosely against Jimmy's knees. That's right. His face was open and vulnerable toward the bony whaps that each somersault gave. The effect was not unlike getting elbowed in the mouth every time you tried a forward roll.

Flip *whack*. Flip *whack*. Flip *whack*.

I would say that Lou took about a good ten shots to the face.

More specifically, to the mouth.

Even *more* specifically, to the front teeth.

By the time the two landed in a heap at the base of the hill, Lou's mouth was a bloody mess (think of a Fourth of July pre-cooked hamburger). John stood at the top, waving and flexing just as I blew the whistle to signal that two minutes had elapsed. The game was over and the crowd, as they say, was going wild. John had won. The twins' strategy had worked. Lou had lost.

And he came up swinging.

His first murderous punch went wild, causing him to sprawl face-first into the side of the hill, and now I saw a mingling of blood and mud, which for reasons I can't explain, reminded me of a caramel and cherry Sundae. Perhaps I hadn't eaten lunch.

The crowd, thinking it was a good-natured gag, cheered appreciatively. Jimmy, however, sensed that Lou was thinking otherwise, and he danced backwards carefully. Lou made another lunge and fell forward, where George and I caught him, held him up and pinned his arms to his side while smiling to the hundreds who were now clapping.

"Lemme go, lemme go," he was muttering through battered teeth.

"Lou," I whispered while still smiling and struggling with him. "You took the chance. You paid the price. You lost the fight."

"Yeah, man," George whispered while waving to the crowd. "Don't lose your kids. Lou, they're watching how you eat crow, dude. They're watching to see how you take losing. I'm begging you. *Don't lose your kids.*"

Lou looked at me through muddy eyes and stopped struggling.

"Lemme go." He shook loose and licked those bloody lips. He turned towards the hundreds of kids.

"I told you," shouted Sally.

"Way to go, Lou," yelled one of the kids from his youth group.

"Smooth moves, Superman," yelled another.

The place fell quiet.

Lou turned slowly and reached for Jimmy. I winced. He grabbed his shirt.

And pulled him towards him and gave him a bear hug.

"You got me, man," he laughed as he pounded on his back. "You got me."

The place erupted in a deafening cheer.

Jimmy returned the hug, and I stood back, listening to the all-male *whump-whump* of back-pounding and realizing another valuable lesson while on my journey.

Lou had been made a complete fool in front of scores of teens. A complete bloody idiot. I know he was in extreme pain, for I believe both his front teeth were cracked, if my memory serves me right. Yet for the sake of his kids, and the scores of teens in that meeting that day, he allowed himself to be abased. Bless him, he swallowed his pride so that the day wouldn't be ruined.

I recall in the book of James the reminder that our Lord gives grace to the humble, and I saw it in living color that day when Lou needed a truckload of grace to keep from ruining his testimony. I thought of the many Christians I had known through the years, and the examples they had shown through humility. The twenty-third chapter of Matthew is a narrative from Jesus Himself in telling us that the ones who choose to be abased will be the ones who finds themselves exalted by Christ.

I looked at Lou in a new light. Here's a fellow who took a beating but laughed it off because of the young kids in his group – many who had not yet become Christians – who needed to see an example of a Christian who could keep the ideals of Jesus.

As that day wrapped up with bedraggled teens filing onto their church's buses, I looked over and saw a group that was still lively and laughing loudly.

It, of course, was Lou's group.

He was surrounded by kids who were escorting him toward their church bus, still cheering for him, patting him on the back and offering him ice cream sandwiches and burgers, which of course he was unable to eat. Sally had calmed down and was even smiling a little. As for Lou, his face was smeared and his lips were swelled painfully, but he was grinning and joking.

I knew that this was a practical display of Godly humility.

Lou had his Godly reactions down pat.

What an example.

What a lesson for me.

14.
Ohio: a Professor with a Servant's Heart, and Yuma's Special Gift

It was the beginning of the summer of 1984 and I was exhausted more than I'd ever been. This past week had been a whirlwind of activities as diverse as I could imagine, including yet another amazing account of God's servants. I had pulled into a Christian college at midnight on Sunday, calling the school and asking only for a place to pillow my head for a few hours. To my amazement, one of the professors met me at the front gate and guided me to his home, where he and his wife provided me with a comfortable family bed. When I got up the next morning, he personally was making my breakfast of oatmeal, eggs and coffee.

Listen to me. This man had a PhD. He had written numerous books. And he was serving *me*, a kid in a broken-down car and two days' worth of grit on his skin. The professor was showing his servant's heart in a quiet and tender way, reminding me that regardless of background or social standing, there are tons of God's people who are kind and often looking for ways to show His love to others.

On Tuesday I was speaking at a church in Gray, Tennessee and along with the speaking schedule, I found time to help out on the host's farm. Mr. Gearson needed me to wrestle down a calf while he took the, uh, necessary steps for castration. I recall having a headlock on the calf, kicking up straw, getting spattered with mud and cow manure, wondering if Saint Augustine ever got himself into situations like this.

Wednesday's journey took me north. I spent three hours talking about Christ to an atheist hitchhiker before dropping him off and speaking at a camp in Kentucky, where part of my ministry was to get involved in a campus-wide water balloon fight. There you have it: from apologetics to soaked underwear, all in one day.

On Thursday I was at another camp with a group of Kentucky teens, and along with my speaking duties the head counselor asked me to organize some water Olympic games, so I spent the day in the pool and the evening in the pulpit. My fingertips showed signs of serious shriveling.

On Friday I was at a camp outside of Columbus, Ohio, where the young adults respectfully asked for a small change in plans. They wanted me to present my evening service in a different way: The folks wanted a literal fireside chat.

"Not behind the pulpit, Brad, not this time," said one young lady. "We want you to sit down next to the bonfire and share something from the Bible in a more casual way."

"Yeah," agreed a fellow next to her, "Share something more down-home."

There were about forty college kids in attendance. As I settled in next to the fire, seated on a wicker chair, a young man named Lloyd spoke up. "Tell us about something when you were a kid. That's be a good place to start," he called.

"Well, okay," I said. "Any special time?"

"Okay, let me think," answered Amanda, "How about a holiday story...Christmas especially? Something from Christmas."

"Yeah," agreed Tammi, "Make your message something from Christmas."

"All right, then," I said, thinking. I liked this unique style of speaking. They were challenging me, and I wanted to be up to the test. "Okay. I'll tell you the story of the holiday after my family had moved to Hershey, Pennsylvania when I was a kid. I can recall the Christmas I wanted to be a ventriloquist."

"A *what*?" asked Roy.

"A guy who throws his voice," I answered. "A guy with a puppet, who's not supposed to move his lips."

"Oh, yeah," said Roy. "I've seen 'em on television."

I continued. "Specifically I wanted to be as good as, or better than Paul Winchell, whom many of you might recognize as Tigger's voice in the Winnie the Pooh cartoons. This guy could make his puppet, whom he called Jerry Mahoney, talk without so much as a flinch of his lips, and I was obsessed with the idea of being able to set up a partner onstage to make wisecracks and witty asides while I played the straight man."

The college students chuckled.

I went on. "Oh, I could see my career take off, especially in my fourth grade class in January, when the teacher, Mrs. Riley, would let anyone march to the front of the class, proudly display one of their Christmas gifts, and chat about it. Why she did this, I don't know - perhaps for the experience of getting in some public speaking. No matter. This was my chance to take center stage and impress the girls, especially Lynette Bredbenner and Lori Morris, two of my dream girls. I had it all planned out: I would show my Jerry Mahoney puppet, go into a routine and make them swoon. Never mind the fact that I was a buck-toothed kid with a long neck and a bad haircut. It's the sheer thespian talent that knocks 'em dead, didn't you know?"

257

The students laughed. "You had buck teeth," chuckled Amanda.

"Yes, well, let's not dwell on that," I said. "Back to the story: I was dropping every hint possible in order to let my mom know that I wanted a Jerry Mahoney puppet more than anything in the world. I was the most anxious kid in the country the week before Christmas. Nothing else seemed to matter but that Jerry Mahoney ventriloquist puppet. I dreamed about using it and speaking without moving my lips. I studied the 'Throw Your Voice' sections of party games books in the Hershey Library. I talked about how I would entertain church groups and school meetings alike. I was obsessed with Christmas morning. And then..." I made a dramatic pause.

"Then what?" asked Robbie.

"The day came," I answered. "I bolted downstairs, along with the rest of my brothers and sisters, to the front room of our country house on Airport Road. Mom had us sit down in front of the tall Christmas tree decked with plastic icicles and spray snow (and I still think spray snow is awesome stuff). We went through the smaller gifts that we exchanged among siblings like car-shaped soaps and boxes of candy canes, and we laughed a lot. It was great. Then ... there was one more present for each child: The Big Gift."

I stopped, for yet another dramatic pause. "One by one we worked our way around the room. I'm telling you, I was in a *sweat*, brother - and I believe I was too young to even have sweat yet - but I can tell you the honest truth, I was shaking whenever I grabbed that wrapping paper. It seems the right size, but you never know..."

"I held the rectangular parcel vertically and I ripped it open halfway up. You know what I saw? Jerry Mahoney peeked through the hole in the wrapping paper."

The college students cheered like middle schoolers.

I nodded. "I shouted, screamed and laughed. I kissed my mom and shouted some more. Christmas Day was *perfect*. Oh, man, what a relief. What a joy! I waited and waited and waited for something so long that I *ached* - and it came to pass." I looked at the students.

"And I look at the life we have right now, and as much as I know things are fun and enjoyable, there is also hurt and grief that we all endure. I *know* there is a better life that God has for us. He's not a monster to make us suffer and then extinguish us from existence. There is a Heaven and I wait anxiously for that day whenever I can see it all come true."

"*For we know that when this earthly tent we live in is taken down-when we die and leave these bodies-we will have a home in heaven, an eternal body made for us by God himself and not by human hands.*"

"We grow weary in our present bodies, and we long for the day when we will put on our heavenly bodies like new clothing. Please understand, we will not be spirits without bodies, but we will put on new heavenly bodies. We want to slip into our new bodies so that these dying bodies will be swallowed up by everlasting life. God himself has prepared us for this, and as a guarantee He has given us the Holy Spirit."

As I closed in prayer and the college students sat by the fire to chat before going off to bed, I thanked the camp counselor and slipped over to my car. There were two envelopes.

One was a gift from the camp, enough to get me to my next destination.

The other was a map that led me to the very last place on my two year circuit. I needed this map.

My meetings had slowed to a standstill, and I knew that God was telling me something in more ways than one. I was dragging myself to the car for the last month. I was spending a lot of times fighting sickness, especially colds. Sleeping in truck stops and trailers wasn't doing anything for my health. I knew that I needed to consider drawing the circuit ministry to a conclusion. When I stopped by my parents' home in Delaware, I told my mother that I was wrapping it up. I had decided that I was going to close down my circuit-riding and look to see how I could enter a new ministry.

Could you believe what happened next?

On the very day that I made my decision, I received a call at my parents' house. The call came from a camp in central Ohio.

"Brad?"

"Yes?"

"Jon Weddington here. How have your travels been going?"

"Fine, Jon. It's going on two years now. Tiring but amazing."

"Well, that's why I wanted to call you. Will you be traveling this summer?"

"Jon," I sat back on the chair. "I'm really not sure."

"Well, then, let me tell you my plans then. Come up here to Ohio. We need you here at our camp. For the whole summer."

"Beg pardon?"

"We want to hire you to be one of our two camp directors. We have one space left and your name came up. You'd be helping lead activities, counseling with all ages of campers, and taking the pulpit

from time to time. You know, I believe it's time for you to get a break from traveling. Would you consider stopping your circuit and being on camp staff?"

God made it clear right at that moment. "Yes, Jon, I'll take it."

So I was heading to Camp Pinefield for the summer. Within the week I was on my last journey, heading to the Buckeye State, envisioning the moment went I entered the campgrounds. I would pull my car up to the leader's cabin and put it in park.

And then I could rest.

"Come to Me, all who are weary and heavy-laden, and I will give you rest." Matthew 11:28

The word *rest* is important to know, because even in the midst of working with two hundred campers a week, I was going to get a time of rest.

The Koine Greek word for "rest" is *anapauo*, and Strong's Concordance says it means "to cause or permit one to cease from any movement or labor in order to recover and collect his strength." That's what I needed to do - collect my strength.

I think one of the most frequent words used by Christians is "busy." We're always filling our calendar with activities like choir, social meetings, group studies, holiday parties, concerts ... and very little time for Jesus Himself.

We need a rest once in a while.

I needed a rest.

I needed *anapauo* - a time to recover my strength and just sit and study more about Jesus while I sat on the cabin porch. The nights would be filled with reflection and Bible reading, not fussing with a map and checking mile markers along Interstate 10.

I loved my circuit, but I knew it was time to make a change. At the camp, I parked the Malibu Classic and gave it a pat. *You get a chance to sit for a while, old friend.*

On the first week I was at camp, we were put into an all-day orientation meeting. The noisy hall was filled with guys and girls ranging in age from late teens to early twenties, laughing and sharing stories of their previous years' college or work adventures. They'd come from all over the country. I looked over and heard one guy say he was from Chicago. Another fellow said he was from Los Angeles. I saw a girl who said she was from Yuma, Arizona. Another guy said he was from Wyoming, near Cheyenne.

I stopped and looked back at the girl from Yuma.

I looked at her for a full minute. From Yuma. I looked at her for another minute.

Suddenly I realized that I wanted very much to get to know about Yuma, Arizona.

The orientation officially started, and the first order of business was to announce assignments. Chicago guy was in charge of crafts. Los Angeles guy was (surprise) a lifeguard. Yuma girl was going to be in charge of the junior girls' cabin.

I decided that I was going to need to learn more about the ministry of this sandy-haired gal who was dedicated of serving the needs of pre-teen girls. Hey, I had two sisters who met that age qualification. *What an ice-breaker.*

Yeah, well, speaking of breaking.

On the second day of camp, we were running through the games the campers would be playing. This was a smart idea, so in having actual experience, we could better acquaint the kids with the various camp competitions.

I was in the middle row of a team volleyball game with other counselors. Since I had been a starter on a college intramural championship team, I felt that this volleyball competition was where I could shine - especially in front of Yuma. For some reason, a short fellow of about seventeen years of age named Davie took a liking to me and hung near me. When I say near me, he stood about eleven inches from me whenever he could. It could have been because his glasses were enormous and his sight was limited, but I didn't know for sure. This crowding issue was also occurring during the volleyball game, and it made for a very cramped situation.

"Oof! Davie, give me some room," I said as he bumped into me bodily for the third time.

"Okay, Brad," he'd say, but end up leaping against me - actually bouncing off me - anytime there was a volley.

Then on the fifth serve, it happened. Davie leaped upward at an angle, using me as a cushion, and he came down – both feet – on the top of my foot. *Crack.*

It almost seemed funny to me, in a weird sort of way; I had spent two years on the road in near-accidents, working on buildings and laboring on farms, ministering in high-crime areas – and yet I'd never been injured. But at the first week of a kids' summer camp, I break my foot. There went my whole summer of playing games. There went my mobility. There may have gone my chance to impress a certain girl from the West. I sat on the camp porch, realizing that this summer would be a pretty rotten situation.

Except that the pretty Yuma girl *also* injured her foot falling off the camp stage during a skit.

Well, what do you know?

Hey, I thought, *both martyrs for the cause.* Heh. What a great opening line.

And I got to meet the girl. I found out her name was not Yuma, but Jill Livesay. We met and talked. And talked and talked. And went to carnivals and apple orchard stands on the weekends. We didn't really walk through the festivals; we both sort of limped along together.

And within two years we were married.

God was good.

He still is.

He led us into new horizons, as I served in broadcast radio, youth work, and other adventures that I hope to share with you in the future. Many of those stories are just as, well, entertaining as the ones in his book.

My circuit riding was over.

But a new life was to begin.

Isn't that just like Him?

When one awesome part of your life hits the end of the trail, our Lord guides you to the start of a new adventurous pathway. It's just another one of the many things I learned about Him on the circuit.

Epilogue:
many thanks to you
for reading my book

I want to thank you for taking the time to read this book. I have had a rollicking good time bringing these memories back to the forefront of my mind and heart, because I'm refreshed whenever I realize that God is a God of blessing and excitement, working miracles every day. I was a front-row witness to them on countless occasions. I was there and I experienced all of this.

I once more want to remind you that I changed some names and places so as not to embarrass anyone.

Or myself any more than I have already.

But what you've just read is an account of the many events that happened during the time when the Lord deigned that I should have a circuit riding ministry around America, so he could both reach *out* to other people and also reach *in* and teach me some important life lessons to further honor Him.

Was this book written to elevate my status among peers? Absolutely not, and I hope you don't get that opinion. I think you can see my many failures, doubts and stumble-bum efforts as I journeyed through the months. I also worked hard to explain the many times the Lord let me know on no uncertain terms that He himself would do the work if I would only step back and let Him take control.

This, in effect, is my *todah* book.

Let me explain. May I share this message from Psalm 116?

I love the LORD, because He hears My voice {and} my supplications.

Because He has inclined His ear to me, Therefore I shall call {upon Him} as long as I live.

Psalm 116 is what is called a Thanksgiving Psalm, and in the Hebrew tongue the word is *todah*. It's an out-and-out exclamation of praise as well as an emotional confession of deep gratitude.

Psalm 18 is another:

He delivered me from my strong enemy,

And from those who hated me, for they were too mighty for me.

They confronted me in the day of my calamity,

But the LORD was my stay.

He brought me forth also into a broad place;

He rescued me, because He delighted in me.

In a *todah* Psalm, you praise God for something He has done for you, and then you offer thanksgiving in the form of worship.

In a *todah* Psalm the wild and cheerful celebration in worship is based on some immediate experience of God's goodness and grace. It's kind of hard to explain, but the word *todah* that we find in these psalms is *much* fuller and deeper than the English word "thanks." It summarizes the singer's explanation of the direct response to prayers of need ("God, please heal my baby", "Father, please help me to finish this work by the deadline", "Lord, please help me to confront the wrongdoer and show love", etc.)

You can see why I call this book a *todah* book. God responded to my prayers. But I also lean upon the other definitions of this beautiful Hebrew word.

It's kind of like an explanation not only of *what* God has done but *why* He did it and *with what authority* He has in doing it.

Todah pinpoints the fact that God is the source of all the great stuff in life. This is a "billboard advertisement" of who He is, and it comes from personal experience as in *"I was there and saw it with my own eyes."*

And, brother, did I ever see it with my own eyes. It was and always will be an amazing time in my life.

Along with writing, I'm now a teacher living in Knoxville, Tennessee with my wife, Jill. Our family has grown to fill out to five with the addition of our three children: Nicholas, Peter and Julianne. As I travel and speak in different places, I get the opportunity of sharing the Bible and God's wondrous ways through the Scripture, how He takes care of us all day by day.

And you know what happens?

Once in while I'm confronted by someone who says "Yes, that's all in the Bible and written down, but have *you* ever had a real *here-and-now* experience with God?"

When that happens, I ask them to sit down and relax.

Because I have quite a few stories to tell them.

ABOUT THE AUTHOR

Brad Zockoll has been a professional writer since 1998, having written for magazines such as *Boys' Life* and Focus on the Family's *Brio* and *Breakaway*. This was his first attempt at non-fiction and anything remotely resembling an autobiography. "I really felt that the years I was on the road were years that helped establish my faith," said Zockoll. "It was amazing to see God working every day in times and places where I was truly alone and had no other help. The more I recalled the stories, the more I had friends tell me that I ought to put them into print. So I did."

Brad Kent Zockoll was born in Pittsburgh, Pennsylvania on May 29, 1959, the fourth of six children. His background primarily includes Christian youth work and teaching, but he also has experience in the fields of radio talk-show and play-by-play sports broadcasting, newspaper column writing, textbook editing and even newspaper cartoon comic strip art.

Brad made a commitment to Jesus Christ in his bedroom at the age of seventeen, and made a decision to follow the Lord in ministry work at the age of twenty.

Brad married Jill Anne Livesay and now lives in Knoxville, Tennessee where he serves as a teacher at Grace Christian Academy. The Zockoll children include Nicholas, Peter and Julianne.

www.ingramcontent.com/pod-product-compliance
Lightning Source LLC
Chambersburg PA
CBHW071953040426
42447CB00009B/1313